Essentialism as a Grand Unifying Theory

Essentialism as a Grand Unifying Theory

Response to *Conflicts in Feminism*

Rebecca Boone

North Atlantic Books
Berkeley, California

Essentialism as a Grand Unifying Theory

ISBN 1-55643-141-4

Published by
North Atlantic Books
2800 Woolsey Street
Berkeley, California 94705

Cover and book design by Paula Morrison
Printed in the United States of America

Essentialism as a Grand Unifying Theory is sponsored by the Society for the Study of Native Arts and Sciences, a nonprofit educational corporation whose goals are to develop an educational and crosscultural perspective linking various scientific, social, and artistic fields; to nurture a holistic view of arts, sciences, humanities, and healing; and to publish and distribute literature on the relationship of mind, body, and nature.

This book is for the love of all I's and you's.

Table of Contents

Introduction

Conflicts in Feminism emphasizes the diversity of conflicting views among academic feminists. Its future on Women's Studies' reading lists seems assuredly bright. The two editors (Marianne Hirsch and Evelyn Fox Keller) and every one of the twenty-two contributors are themselves professors with impressive positions on the university level. The Introduction, Conclusion, and Coda of the editors are incisive and undefensive. While their announced commonality rests on the admittedly regrettable facts that both are American, white, middle class, heterosexual, academic, Jewish, and *women*, it was not revealed whether or not the editors are both *mothers*. In my book, motherhood would be the primary and possibly the only commonality worth examining as a ground upon which to structure "*feminist theory.*"

As a descriptive term, "theory" is so overworked throughout the book as to be virtually useless. Several of the articles question its use. Theories, from astronomy and physics to political and cultural "theories" of social "norms" must ultimately rely upon confirmable observations of natural entities. These articles appear prone to tie in abstract notions such as equality, freedom, human rights, class, difference, science, and criticism itself, especially criticism surrounding deconstruction and psychoanalysis as methodologies. If mentioned at all in these essays, motherhood along with womanhood appears as rather a curse if not an outright and quite unnecessary evil. Gender itself is grudgingly admitted as something everyone is conscious of, but nowhere is gender used as the criterion of one's identity, social function, and self-understanding.

These academic feminists seem to be gunning for an autonomous Personhood, except for the lone male contributor,

Thomas W. Laqueur, whose unquestioned male autonomy reaches out for logical assurance that his fatherhood somehow makes him a legitimate co-parent with the person who bore "his" child. Laqueur's is the only article that can be said to argue for *the essentiality of male authority* from the venerable analytical *theory* as found in Graeco/Judaic/Christian theological philosophies.

In my view, feminists must do a sounder logical analysis of the situation than this, and a better job of writing it up, if there's to be any *theoretical* contest whose outcome decides *whether the mothers or their male children* are expected to: run our governments and social institutions; determine our cultural ceremonies and traditions; sit as judges over our morality and ethics. Shall the governance of men be on the shoulders of men, or shall it be on the shoulders of the mothers who bear and care for men? Of course it would be lovely if men took upon their shoulders the responsibilities of caring for women and children, as advertised. However, that would be to expect the unusually sensitive male child to be *able* to fulfill his often expressed desire to care for the mother and his siblings. Biologically, our appearance and disappearance in space-time don't function in such a way that learned children may helpfully instruct mothers concerning the facts of life. Philosophers and feminists alike need to take more careful note of life's sequences and consequences.

There's more to be said for essentialism than feminists have yet reasoned out. *Conflicts in Feminism* serves as evidence that, still following the lead of masculinist theologies, feminists are busy denying any identity with their biological fate of functioning existentially as a sexual system. Yet it remains a fact that gender identity encompasses both biological *and social* aspects of our being. Men long since figured this out, and that is why they denied identity with their paltry sexual act and switched to man's mighty *mind* as the "function" according to which man is properly identified. What man's mighty mind tells him is that woman is indispensable to his survival; to work out a social system to his liking, he must control woman, else the jig is up and he will be bound to obey woman and fit into *her* constructions of social norms. Nowhere in *Conflicts in Feminism* is there the least hint that woman is irreparably stuck with a biological *function and identity*, as indeed also is man. Instead, denial is rampant and takes many silly and tedious forms. Unfortunately, these denials likely will be music to the ears of young ladies enrolling in Women's Studies at the university level who are longing also for the male ideals of freedom and self-determination.

The essentialism that I feel feminism must defend as its *theoretical* answer to man's *theory* of himself (which absurd theory is succinctly presented and I'm afraid seriously argued by Laqueur) is rooted in motherhood as a biological fact. Fatherhood is also a biological fact but, as I said, it is not upon the male sexual act per se that the theory rests. It rests rather upon the supposed capacity of the male to create form out of woman's supposedly formless materiality. In other words, for man, the child is an *idea*, something he *imagines*. Only out of man's imagination can a [male] child, under the father's tutelage, be molded into a decidedly civilized, human being of heroic character and godlike attributes. (In man's theory of man and mankind, woman remains in her function as biological babymaker, reproducing herself for future mothering functions, and sons for glorification as the father, the son, and the holy god.) Through writing, men have cleverly if not maliciously woven this laughable theory of fatherhood through every social fabric of every culture of today's human world. Man's theory of himself as lord and master of woman and the human race is most flamboyantly applied in the commercial and political "worlds" of men; but the truth is, the human world is one world. In what we do physically, sexually, and culturally there are no boundaries between public and private affairs. Neither are there races among us; we are one specific race, one specific humanity.

The way to knock man's theory of himself out of our social institutions and citadels of learning is to displace it with a better and demonstrably more accurate theory of motherhood.

There is a set of persons classifiable as mothers, based on what they *do*, but there is no set of persons classifiable as fathers, based on what they *do*. Fatherhood is a trumped up and rather new term. The set of persons classifiable as males is properly assigned to the category "sons." Thus, any discursive efforts to dredge up a workable theory of feminism must first establish definite objects that the theory applies to, and categorically these are just two: mothers and sons. As I've often said, all girls are little mothers and all boys are little fuckers. Once the terms are understood, the theory must elucidate the dynamics of how the entities in question relate to each other *dynamically*, and that means *sexually.* "We" is one body, female in its identity as determined by the mother's sexual functions; she alone bears offspring in her own likeness as well as a member also in her likeness called the son who has no capacity to bear offspring. As members of our mother's body, males must remain employable and useful to the species woman.

If the logically false theory of fatherhood is not soon displaced by a logically correct feminist theory of motherhood, that which is specifically human (and clearly derived from the human mother's intelligent identification of herself as mother, and sovereign over men at all times) will perish if indeed it hasn't already. Feminism is far from establishing itself as both a *religion* (the truth that binds) and a *philosophy* (the extenuation of religious truth coloring all of our cultural values). Feminism has no choice but to be grounded squarely on the *necessary governance* of men by women as a result of *logical analysis of biology alone.* The religious philosophy of fatherhood is solidly grounded on the "necessary" governance and control of women by men as both logical and factual *in theory,* albeit this metaphysical theory absolutely contradicts easily observable facts. Civil, economic and psychological independence for *mothers* was rejected in Greece as in Judaism, Christianity, and Islam *because* men correctly reasoned that if left rich and free, woman does not hesitate to enjoy her own sexual proclivities as well as to structure her own social institutions and the ethical values of her children according to her own tastes. In a feminist theory of woman and womankind, woman must remain in her immutable office where she functions as authoritative babymaker. In this official capacity, she reproduces herself in two modes: female and male.

Any theory of woman or man as being separable from the mother's *specific* sexual, two-gendered system will be false, I believe. Our specific sexual system is obviously represented by maternal functions, since those functions include the production of the son, also called father when in his maturity he copulates with woman. Man's connection with his mother is thought of as being asexual but that is clearly a puritanical refusal to view the mother's acts of gestation, parturition, and breast feeding as sexual acts. One purpose of female sexuality is to keep woman's male members bound to the female's reproductive system: the important gene packet he carries must be returned to the system for its own use. The complaint of many feminists seems to be that the system's own biological methodology for holding the species together not only serves to "oppress" woman, but, they "explain," *because* of the demands sexuality makes upon females, the female biological system itself must be rejected and denied as in any way representative of woman's true Self.

Autonomy is a big buzzword now, but as a fact it is delusional. Free will and intention are other treacherous terms, largely delusional in that we kid ourselves in terms of what our body's intentions really are; the "will" of every body is appetitive and normally sexual. What women have in common is an identical body, and so it is with men. I think feminist claims that such things as race, color, and culture divide us (other than in trivial ways) are total bunk. The commonality of woman and man is our mother. Theory, as Keller of all people would know, is a scientific term. If feminism dedicates itself to a logical analysis of the existential *function* of woman as *mother of womankind* (within whose systemic body man is embraced just as the written word shows), the appropriate descriptive term is not "doing theory" but doing philosophy. Theories can be tested; philosophy can only be discussed and adjudicated by personal opinion using personal observation and experience as reference. The experiences, observations, and opinions of mothers have never been made a part of discursive philosophy, written up and published by would-be authoritative sons to the exclusion of more authoritative mothers. *Conflicts in Feminism* does little to remedy this imbalance, for as one author states, "feminism is about tenure" mostly.

Feminism seems to have begun as a general stirring or reawakening of woman's consciousness. Suddenly *mothers* have become aware of and deeply shocked by what our sons are doing. Deep down, *the maternal system knows* that the male member which evolved out of the systemic Self (i.e., the very Self that is synonymous with Mother, which is the same Self as the originary Subject "I") must be used and exploited to serve *the maternal system*. The system's male member cannot be allowed to become the system's ruin and of course it goes without saying that there cannot be *two* specific systems in the one and only human world bound by its unified blood, our genetic consanguinity. We are one race.

The very essence of essentialism is the human mother's knowledgeable acceptance of her biological fate and her *determination in view of this knowledge* to make her own life and the life of her progeny more comfortable, safe, and less monotonous and boring, more *entertaining*. She accomplished all of this through her intelligence, educating and ruling her offspring with an imaginative, benign, and civilized hand. The human mother at no point considers herself better or above dumb animals. She knows that she is only more cognizant of the way things work than they appear to be (and we could be wrong about this; it may be a matter of language). Man's tyranny of woman is neither benign nor civilized; in fact, it is now observably beneath the natural dignity of dumb animals. This is the tyranny of the willful male child. It is the function of the human mother to civilize her children and to expect the process to work the other way around is logical lunacy.

Feminism must move towards discursive philosophy and logic, now that mothers have learned to read and write as effectively as sons. Relentless analyses and arguments from *the mother's physical point of view* must be stacked against the feeble metaphysics of wistful but also physically and intellectually willful sons. After all, if one is born male, what are one's options after discovering that one cannot physically follow in the beloved mother's footsteps?

Feminist philosophy perhaps faces a real handicap in the fact that mothers in general do *not* have inquiring minds. Imagination and gift for artistry are different in temperament and intellectual focus from scientific inquiry and determination *to know*. Mothers in general have extremely inventive pragmatic minds usually focused on the economics and pleasures of *community* survival. By amusing us children, our human mothers teach us to laugh. We mothers do not waste precious energy worrying about our identity, who we are, where we come from, what we are for, or whether or not there is certainty of any knowledge worthy of all men to be believed. Those are the questions of prepuberty children. It is understandable that men ask them all their lives long, since they are never forced by fate into that dreaded and burdensome adulthood which motherhood alone coerces females into comprehending, figuring out in some detail, and finally (being superintelligent creatures), *accepting* as immutable facts. These are neither lamentable nor inglorious facts, as many of today's anti-essentialism feminists seem to have concluded.

Although many women might elect to do so, woman as mother cannot abdicate her sovereign fate, despite the seemingly unfair and intolerable fact that only woman gets saddled with responsible adulthood while man keeps his irresponsible child-like freedom. Yes, bearing children is oppressive and burdensome, yet out of sheer intelligence and imagination the human mother and no "other" once structured the specific family lifestyle that bears our species' name: human. Before human mothers gird themselves once again to structure a better life for ourselves as well as everyone else, *true feminists* must displace the false theory of fatherhood, now prevailing in "human" cultures, with an unassailable analysis of the essential biological system that makes the mother sovereign over her male members through all eternity. Only a dumb alpha male would expect or want it to be otherwise.

1

Ann Snitow tells us that

> . . . a common divide keeps forming in both feminist thought and action between the need to build the identity "woman" and give it solid political meaning and the need to tear down the very category "woman" and dismantle its all-too-solid history. Feminists often split along the lines of some version of this argument, and that splitting is my subject.

Snitow is observant and insightful, but she has the wrong divide under scrutiny. The constantly recurring divide is between motherhood and childhood, which is to say between adulthood and childhood. Eternal sisterhood can be questioned for the same reasons eternal brotherhood can; neither is necessarily connected with the responsibilities and brute facts of biological maturation. Everyone knows that childhood is not eternal. The question "Is motherhood eternal?" is more easily answered "Yes" than is the question concerning fatherhood. Without motherhood, childhood is unimaginable, but maternal systems that do not rely upon a dynamic employing two distinct genders are easily cited. Motherhood understood as that function which forces the female from childhood to adulthood can be neither minimized nor maximized. Function is what function does and so we look first to an entity's possible function in order to arrive at its correct identity. The female as mother functions throughout all biological life forms free of evaluations of its comparable or incomparable worth: no mother, no offspring, no species.

The divide between entities is always a matter of space-time. As applied to human beings, the divide is between generations; put most succinctly, the divide is between mothers and offspring. While the agency of mothers is all-encompassing, it is not primarily a political or discursive agency. The agency of feminism can neither build the identity woman in order to give it solid political meaning, nor can it tear down the very category woman and dismantle its "all-too-solid history." [Is Snitow inferring that woman's history is all too reprehensible, or what?] Feminists like Snitow are right in surmising that our species' current social structures can and should be radically modified; but fooling around with the identity of woman as mother and disavowing the profundity of the mother's biological functions will get feminism nowhere.

As mother, woman is at once economic system, font of all goodness, mentor, defender, namer of all things, judge, confessor, absolver of our transgressions, inventor of rituals and ceremonies that civilize, entertain, and keep us bound socially together. In their early, dependent years, *children* are prone to idealize their mother, but the mother is not in the least inclined to idealize herself or her function; she wishes with all her heart that such arduous duties were not required of her, and she looks for ways to abdicate her office with its overwhelming and thankless duties. When sons step forward offering help, using delegated authority over younger siblings and eventually relieving the mother of her community responsibilities as well, the arrangement looks like a lifesaver to the exhausted and overextended mother. Over time, this arrangement of sons functioning for mothers on the basis of a delegated authority put so much economic control in the hands of men that the authentic authority of the mothers was forgotten or legislated out of existence.

This most disruptive of all social divides—that between the authentic authority of mothers and the inauthentic authority of sons—Snitow entirely misses. Her poignant section on motherists versus feminists (grief-stricken Argentine mothers whose children have been murdered versus the murderous Argentine male State) does not touch the root of the matter. Not yet has a single collectivist movement nor a single feminist "theory" correctly based whatever feminist logic it laid claim to on the natural, authentic authority of mothers. The sons' usurpation of the authority of mothers is what the tyranny of men over women is all about. But if, in every succeeding generation pseudo authority is handed to sons on a platter, how can we blame the sons for sacralizing it in canon law and legitimizing it in the secular?

2

Nancy E. Cott's historical perspectives on the Equal Rights Amendment recount what I see as the confusion of another false divide. It is absurd to set a goal of enabling women to have the same opportunities and situations as men, the reason being that mothers and children categorically have different situations and "opportunities." During childhood, girls and boys may be presented with "equal" opportunities and situations in much larger measure than has heretofore been done, but ultimately feminist philosophy must be pitted against the theology of masculinist philosophy. The former holds that, based on biological functions, mothers are the authentic holders of all offices of authority; the latter holds that, based on metaphysics and divine "law," sons are the rightful holders of all offices of authority. As for civil "rights," those are strictly determined by the legislators who are placed in offices of authority for the purpose of legislating social activities. There is no intrinsic reason why mothers and daughters as well as sons could not be "elected" to legislative office, but I am convinced that there are deep psychological reasons why women will find it difficult to win such elections. Women are comfortable delegating authority to men (see above). Women have never acquired the habit of delegating authority to daughters since it is obvious that authentic authority is bestowed with the advent of the daughter's own motherhood. Most mothers find it entirely satisfactory for brothers, uncles, spouses, sons, and lovers to run public affairs and deal in commerce while they stay home and create beautiful estates of civilized social intercourse. It makes no sense at all to label men oppressor or "enemy," and feminism will gain no ground by sticking to such a hue and cry.

Like labor unions for men, an equal rights amendment for working women is a product of an outdated Calvinist work ethic. Karl Marx's patchwork analysis of this travesty of human endeavor can be respected. A feminist analysis, however, must reappraise the makeup of the family and the centrality of the mother and her authority over sons in a way that the chauvinist Marx was entirely incapable of doing. As terrified as men are at the specter of woman achieving economic independence, for they correctly see that sexual independence goes hand in hand with it, feminists can force legislators to *support mothers and children* whether or not they are interested in entering the work force. Most women enter the work force out of desperate economic need to feed a family and pay the rent. It is the function of every civilized community to take care of its mothers; the best is none too good for these bearers of our life. For feminists to concentrate on what females should *earn* in the marketplace diverts too much attention (and energy) from fundamental philosophical questions of woman's incomparable biological worth and essential authentic authority.

3

Mary Childers and Bell Hooks take up the red herrings of race and (social) class. Again, these feminists overlook *mothers* as the set of individuals that any feminist theory must point to. "We both use a yardstick whittled from early experience of poverty to measure definitions of oppression and claims of universality," they state. I would counter that it is the mother's experience of parturition that produces children as *oppressive* but unblameworthy. Certainly, extreme poverty increases the feeling of oppression for such mothers, but social malfunctions must be kept separate from feminist theory. Feminism is not about women but about motherhood and the dominance of female biology, just as male dominance is about the metaphysical exaltation of fatherhood. Again, the "classes" that must be kept in mind are the class of mothers and the class of children. The difference in *theory* turns on the question of authority, who commands authority, the mother or the "father." Unquestionably it is the mother, the "father" being categorically the son who is born and lives under the dominion of the mother's jurisdiction. Rites of passage of course are prevalent to remove males from the mother's dominion and jurisdiction but that is just one artifice among many that men have devised to co-opt and to hold for themselves the offices of authority that over time were delegated to them by mothers.

The governance of sons is the biggest question feminists have to discuss. Cultural and religious values as well as the psychology of sexual control of one gender by the other enter with force into any such discussions. Instead of race and class understood as referring to color and poverty lines, feminism must dig deeper and think of race as our unified human species and class as the set of mothers who represent our species. Universally, we experience ourselves daily as human, adult or child, female or male. The catch is that females and males who are not classifiable "mothers" must be assigned to the "children" category, for there are just two categories that are *physically connected:* mothers and children. The intricacies of how these two categories are logically and physically connected are the stuff of feminist theory and of philosophy and theology as well; one must find oneself in one or the other category and understand what *function* being there entails. Language is more or less secondary, and how we *feel* about any of it is almost totally irrelevant. Socially, attitude and behavior may appear to matter, but what really matters is what the specific sexual system *does* by way of keeping itself intact. The mother's sexual system is faltering as a result of the social (and political) systems man has implemented for his own selfish pleasures. Essentialism will change all of that as it becomes better understood and the authentic and natural authority of mothers becomes more assertive. The biological system itself of course remains constant in its two-gendered way of doing things.

4

Katie King claims to be exploring "the shifting feminist politics of sexual preference from three directions." She lists these as: "Sex Debates," "Theory in Press," and the "Apparatus for the Production of Feminist Culture." King shrewdly asks us to note "what counts as theory and for whom." I had already noticed in my first swift overview of *Conflicts in Feminism* that there was no theory offered that would address or accommodate my arguments for the essentialism of motherhood. King's focus on lesbianism as a situational difference is self-centered and I would argue irrelevant to any theory dealing with biological "norms," defined as that which is most effective and dynamic in structure and function—physically as well as culturally. Lesbianism and male homosexuality are embroiled in the non issue of how one *feels* about being female or male. There is no place in theory for *feeling*. How a mother feels about her child is also irrelevant; it is how she performs her duty to the child that counts. Here is where human intelligence becomes the crucial factor in determining what makes our species human: the human mother suddenly *recognizes* her child as her former and future Self. This is not so much a feeling as an epiphany. From that point forward, a distinguishable human species exists. This epiphany is far from guaranteeing that all human mothers will function more admirably than dumb mothers, that is, mothers lacking human language. It does guarantee that the fear and loathing of being female, and, in the son's case, the resentment and jealousy of *not* being female, are psychological realities to be reckoned with when it comes to the performance of one's biological and social duties.

The magnitude of the difference between being female or male has yet to be comprehended by the mother, for she sees her offspring, be they girls or boys, as two modes or models of herself; and so they are, but the logical (and mathematical) complexities of how they work together are enormous. Feminism will not introduce a new age of fresh thought until we are able to state a working hypothesis that takes into account the pervasive sexuality of the female system which produces male members as a property of herself. The hypothesis must explain how the originary female system succeeded in using its property to benefit itself, which is to say, the human species. With the hypothetical situation stated and its logical implications understood, we can then observe the system and collect our scientific data by observing and properly annotating the biological essentialism of motherhood as manifested in a system thoroughly conscious of itself as it goes about performing its bounden duties. Obviously, it is the human mother's *conscious* performance of her often unpleasant duties that civilizes us and makes our world human. Is the human world a better world than the animal world? That is the question. When the intelligent human mother is in charge, I think it is; when the "father" is allowed to run things, human life may become much worse than the lives of speechless animals. Data showing widespread personal preferences for sons no doubt reflect religious biases favoring males. Many mothers, however, remain strong in independent thought while outwardly conforming to cultural and religious tyrannies out of desperate economic necessity. And don't forget that all human *instruction* is some form of brainwashing. If feminism gets the *right* word out, it will flourish over time and eventually the *true* word, which is the mother's word and not the father's, will become canonical.

King grapples with the complexities she sees as "differences": race, class, nationality, language, religion, ability, as well as "too many genders" and "sexualities." I would point out that all of these converge in the essentialism of motherhood, a notion largely ignored or disdained among academic and lesbian theorists. From what I read, the most significant news coming from lesbians is their desire to function as mothers, to "have" families. I agree with King that the structures of power which promulgate "successful" theories (and social values) exhibit themselves in academia alongside commercially successful writing functioning under the rubric "publish or perish." One can only observe shades of Thomas Kuhn's "The Structure of Scientific Revolutions." I would like to agree with King in concluding that "reified 'theory' in the academy depends upon communities *theorizing*," but I am uncomfortable doing so (her emphasis). Reified theory in the academy seems rather to depend upon regular paychecks arriving for the professors who have been successful in publishing all sorts of nonsense. In my book, theory refers to the function of materiality, but the desirability of economic security must be kept separate from theorizing about the mother's material biological function, her mater-ality. The *truth* of mothers as a *function* is so obvious and I would say well *understood* by those who *do* it, that to theorize about its dynamics seems absurd. However, the powerful effectiveness of publishing over millennia an insupportable (because it's *wrong*) interpretation of the mother's essential truth forces us to publish and teach a radically different interpretation. This new feminist *canonical* teaching must *displace* the old, wrong one. Feminists can scarcely be expected to teach what we don't yet have, namely, a *doctrine* of our own, a counter-teaching to what has for so long been taught and canonically accepted, namely, the false "theory" that the essentialism of the father supersedes the essentialism of the mother.

King ends her paper with the observation that "challenges to what counts as theory are still needed." I am offering not only a challenge to what feminists are counting as "theory," but a genuine theory based on physics, logic, and observable existential reality. One can only observe that all of the constituent factors in lesbian theory that King invokes—sexual repressions and license, proliferating sexualities/ethnicities, "new" genders, "new" sex, restatements and mixtures of sexuality and identity, new "mestizas" describing a third category, written genres of theoretical interventions, destabilizing theoretical tools of poststructuralist thought, and a multitude of theorizing communities producing "intersecting conversations"—do not a baby make.

5

Peggy Kamuf's short paper (six pages) raises by far the profoundest questions in the book. She uses a quote from Foucault to lay her base: "Man is an invention which the archaeology of our thought can easily show to be of recent date. And perhaps to be nearing its end." Kamuf suggests that when thought moves beyond the limits of what has made it possible to think "man" as an autonomous whole, the process of ending has begun. The identification of human with masculine, she further suggests, is precisely what feminist scholars have set out to expose and to rectify. Then comes the first question: If one can accept how and why Western thought about human form has taken the shape it has, then can one also conclude that modifying that shape to include feminine contours will result in something fundamentally different? She presses on: Where does feminist theory get its faith in the form of the questions it asks to get at truth if not from the same central store that supplies humanism with its faith in *the universal truth of man*? (My emphasis.) She gives examples of the form of questions feminists ask: What is women's language, literature, style, or experience?

Another most penetrating question is: What if the power of [male] power structures is sustained and even extended by such notions as "getting at the truth of the object"? This is the question which Foucault asks and by way of answer he discerns, behind codified procedures for increasing knowledge about "man" in all his many aspects, a growing technology of control and a proliferation of instruments of power. One result is that science historically has operated with the notion of a norm, in partnership with institutions which enforce social norms by means of exclusion and internment—asylums, prisons, juvenile homes, hospitals, and not least, schools. What touches feminist theory in Foucault's analyses, Kamuf points out, is that [male] power has pursued its aim of social control through a proliferation of institutions that may be understood as manifestations of the "humanistic" self-knowledge of males.

Kamuf's own observation is that [male] power and [male] self-knowledge maintain a highly ambiguous relationship which nevertheless gets articulated in social institutions. I cannot help but respond instantly with the suggestion that the mother's authentic *authority* coupled with self-awareness of her agency of motherhood unfortunately has no current articulation in extant social institutions controlled by men. Kamuf seems to be asking if there is within feminist criticism a "knowledge about women" which has been excluded by masculine-dominated ideology disguised as universal humanism. She stresses that to reach "...the authentic and essential human (as opposed to masculine) truths *of literature* may have an appeal as a theoretical program precisely *because* it replicates the familiar dream of humanism: a single center of truth to which all representation refers." (My emphasis.) To which the essentialist must reply, Yes! Except these humanistic truths are *not* found in literature or holy writ, but in the self-immolation of motherhood, motherhood being the one institution founded by Nature rather than power-hungry, punitive man.

But Kamuf does not stop here with her hard-driving questions. She pursues possibilities with this conditional question: If feminist theory can be content to propose cosmetic modifications on the face of humanism *and its institutions,* will it have done anything more than reproduce the structure of woman's exclusion in the same [male] code which has been *extended* to include her? (My emphasis.) The essentialist's answer is No. The reason is that feminism is more than petitioning for a better deal from the old man. The male code is undone and devastated the moment the mother raises her voice authoritatively *with the expressed intent* of withdrawing the previously delegated authority from her male members. Not incidentally, essentialist humanism as manifested in motherhood has no established social institutions at the moment. That is why I insist that it is imperative for academic feminists to speak and lecture *as mothers*. Those who insidiously protect or openly defend the authority and name of the father will not be recognized as *feminists* but rather as old-guard chauvinists and masculinists.

Kamuf next switches interestingly to the aesthetics of consciousness with a quote from Josephine Donovan, whose writings I am unfamiliar with. However, I would offer a paraphrase: until we begin to codify *the patterns of consciousness of our human mothers*, we will be unable to develop a substantial feminine aesthetic or an adequate feminist social theory, which ideally must complement each other. I might add that such data, to be valid, must reflect patterns of consciousness of *economically independent* mothers. Economic impoverishment can make anyone a "Rice Christian" or aesthetician.

As we all know, Foucault's analysis ends with the end of man as the central object of thought but Kamuf seems to miss a great opportunity for feminist criticism here. The end of man would be the end of man's glorification of himself as a godlike super creature. The strength of Foucauldian discourse is that it situates itself outside the humanist enterprise and envisions the end of humanistic goals currently metaphysically grounded in a male godhead and discourse with "Him." The point which neither Foucault nor Kamuf considers is that the male child's thoughts have no way of attaining human content to the same extent or on the same basis as the mother's thoughts, for sheer lack of the experience of motherhood. It should not be overlooked that in large measure the drama of

Christ's crucifixion and resurrection emulates the passion, self-immolation, and suffering of every mother. The mother has never glorified herself except as a lowly agent doing the obscure work of an entity unimaginably larger and more glorifiable than anything she can personally understand. For highly evolved woman, this "entity" is the omnipresent, all-powerful Nature that surrounds her in space-time, an entity she correctly sees as properly controlling her own life and function. A phallocentric religion's co-option of this becoming posture and religion's perverse interpretation of nature's subjugation of woman as subjugation by a divine phallus are scarcely the fault of motherhood itself.

I cannot agree with Kamuf when she concludes that "... what feminist thought can and has put in question is the capacity of any map to represent more than a fiction of the world's contours." One has only to think motherhood when one reads feminism to catch Kamuf and others in many indefensible statements. Motherhood is not a fiction, nor is it a discourse. Motherhood is about doing the regenerative thing quite beyond any creature's control; the human mother is an agreeable, *knowing* agent. When it comes to man doing his regenerative thing, he is *not* an agreeable or willing agent: he decisively intends to control his physical attraction to and desire for the mother. It can be argued that the only way that man can be unified with Nature is to be reconciled with woman as his authority, mentor, and judge. This he has consistently resisted doing. Unfortunately for everybody, what feminist thought can and has so far put in question is the capacity of any biological mother to represent more than a dull version of the human world's contours. This is precisely what male thought put into question: self-sacrifice is dull, altruism is dull, identification with children is dull, housekeeping is dull, in fact, civilization itself is dull: mayhem and violence are more fun. This attitude and its attendant behavior may be psychologically a simple-minded but jealous and covetous male reaction to the mother's accomplishments and especially to her office of authority: If I can't be "it," if I can't do "it," then nobody shall be or do what I have no capacity to be or do: a real dog-in-the-manger attitude.

I don't know about feminist theory, but woman's nervous system is not focused on a totalizing quest to know herself or to "explain" the universe according to dreamed up scientific "laws." The mother's conscious knowledge of her Self is in unity and oneness with her understanding of who her Self is (mother and host to life) and what her Self is for (to suffer and to bear life, to let it be). In harmony with the difficulties of functioning in space-time, the mother sees little if any difference between "inside" and "outside," the private and the public, the known and the unknown. She views Nature as never less than friend: never so calm that it cannot become violent, and never so violent that it will never be calm. The fixity of every mother's situation is her connection with the natural forces found in space-time itself, and these cannot be different in kind from the forces within the enclosing limits of any female womb-world which produces her Self and all progeny. To my mind, only essentialism with its all-encompassing functions of motherhood can serve as a basis for an inclusive theory of existential reality which is referentially accurate. Like Kamuf, I am left to conclude from necessity: the necessity not "... of replacing this discourse with another and of finding always another place from which to begin...," but the necessity of replacing each mother with another and of finding always a succeeding mother with whom to begin afresh, with renewed energy, the exciting business of doing nature's own most glorious work. Nature does not need our help; it is every creature's glory to participate as best it can, and it could well be argued that the most heinous acts of men serve and glorify Nature as effectively as any suffering mother. I personally would doubt such an argument since many of man's vilest acts (in war, for instance) are committed in the name of glorifying an almighty male divinity who is understood as demanding craven worship along with worldly tribute. That still leaves a plethora of depraved acts against woman and her images that defy explanation or excuse except under the plea of insanity.

One is forced to consider the dismaying possibility that the energized forces of Nature by which nature keeps itself going do not distinguish between sane and insane acts.

6

In her short article, Nancy K. Miller says that for the purposes of argument she will align herself "with those on the side of what Peggy Kamuf in these pages calls 'corrections'; with those who wish to 'rectify or reverse woman's exclusion' without... taking the proper measure of the *epistemological* dangers implicit in such a position.... I will speak as one who believes that 'we women' must continue to work for the woman who has been writing, because not to do so will reauthorize our oblivion."

My position and argument is that we *mothers* must continue to work for the woman who mothers, as must *society as a whole*, for not to do so assures humanity's oblivion. Mothers notoriously do not look after or care for themselves. Surely, it is a sign of intelligence that women viewing motherhood ask, "What's in it for me?" Seeing nothing but a dismal life of self-negation, many might turn away if given a choice. Such a choice might soon result in humanity's demise. The essentiality of mother and motherhood to a *human species* cannot be simply glossed. As a *human* culture, how everybody understands the societal *function* of mothers and motherhood is the single question of most import to feminism, philosophy, religion, and logic. This understanding must be based upon material facts sans metaphysical "explanations" or psychological feelings.

I am not a literary person and find feminists who orient their feminism to literary figures less than forthcoming with respect to their own viewpoints. The *Portuguese Letters* and The *Story of O* which Miller finds so engrossing are far removed from any theory of feminism incorporable within the essentialism of motherhood. It takes considerable perseverance on my part to read carefully feminist writing that is inspired by Derrida, Lacan, or other deconstructionists and psychoanalysts, and I would not do it except that these writings seem to me a small advance over feminist writing inspired by masculinist religions, for instance, the "essentialism" of Mary Daly.

Miller heads her article with a Derridean quote: "I will go so far as to risk this hypothesis: The sex of the addresser awaits its determination by or from the other. It is the other who will perhaps decide who I am—man or woman. Nor is this decided once and for all. It may go one way one time and another way another time."

Typically, Derrida has it about one-fourth right. What I *do* decides what I am, and it is true that I may *appear* to be doing one thing at one time and another thing at another time. For example, at one time I may *appear* to be "doing" an egg and at another time I may appear to be "doing" a chicken, but whatever I appear to be doing, I am unified and systemically whole, else I could do nothing. But who is this other and what does the other do that in any way concerns my Self and what I am doing at any given time? What is this sex that awaits its determination by the other? If sex describes something I do, is the sex I do therefore determined by this functionally undefined other? The most that can be said concerning this case, it seems to me, is that the *reaction* of an other indicates not who I am but *what* I am to *it*. Nor apparently is this decided once and for all; but a close inspection of switcharoos may in fact help us discern a quite stationary pattern. For instance, the once indispensable mother is viewed by the semigrown child as being anything but indispensable. The pubescent girl who passionately loves her father as well as the boy who loves the mother both learn to redirect their passion onto the same objects, categorically speaking, but known by other names and encountered as other persons. Also significantly, these same but differently labeled persons turn out to be needed in other places and at other times. It should not be too difficult to see that sweetheart or wife in place of mother, and lover or husband in place of father, does not change the essential paradigm of mother and child. It is somewhat easier to see that a boy's need for the sweetheart mother and his eventual need for a sexual sweetheart, like the girl child's need for a sweetheart mother and her eventual need for a sexual sweetheart, do not represent a simultaneous neediness. In short, the mother *categorically* is ubiquitous in every phase of the systemic sequencing of her continuing self. Children, also ubiquitous, are but manifestations (at times analogous to eggs) of changing phases of motherhood's all-encompassing form and principle.

Apropos of feminism's criticism of the adequacy of a masculine identity to represent the universal, Miller issues a wonderful caveat to her sister theorists. Don't be too confident, she warns, that nondiscursive practices will respond correctly to the correct theory of discursive practice. If there is anything that is nondiscursive and yet intimately related to any possible feminist theory, it is motherhood. Miller gives "feminist rewritings of literary history" the credit for radically questioning the adequacy of maleness as representing the universal. This seems too removed from any possible application to the observable, physical facts upon which feminism must ultimately justify itself. It is not femaleness nor maleness that presents the universal, but *motherhood* and its implied continuum of functions and duties. Fatherhood nowhere near covers such an implied continuum in its function or social duties. Moreover, neither masculinity nor femininity are appropriate universals, as many have pointed out, but *mother* is not only an identity that overtakes every woman who becomes a mother, *motherhood* is a universal *instituted by* the universal *function* of woman as mother. In no similar way can fatherhood be thought of as a universal instituted by the universal function of man as father, the chief reason being that man's deposit of semen does not leave a viable mark comparable to the mother's deposit of a child. Man's incapacity to leave a vital sign *in space-time* also demonstrates the male's lack of systemic integrity; men are more correctly seen and described as male members, or property, of the female system. To remain viable, the vitality of male semen must be deposited in the *system* from which its gene packet derived. The integrity of the singular system, which is always female, depends upon the use for herself of those properties which evolved out of her functioning self. In short, it is not the sexual act of coitus or copulation that determines parenthood, but woman's parturition where depositor and depositee first experience distance in space-time. Multiple extrusions from the mother's inviolable dynamic can never destroy or weaken her wholeness, however many depraved and villainous, cancerous and debilitating, mutants may appear along with the healthy. Though she die, the integrity of the mother's oneness forever lives and her continuous resurrection is assured.

In the *Portuguese Letters,* the plaintiff Nun makes her lovelorn plea, "Tell me that you want me to die of love for you!" Miller asks with some urgency, If "dying of love" is a trope, what is it a trope of? I can answer that. It *is* a trope and it alludes to the universal paradigm of mother and child which every love (read sexual) situation parodies, including coitus. *You* (the child of parturition) always desires, demands, and expects *I* (the suffering subject mother) to die of love for *you*. The sex-starved Nun is begging this guy to let her function as his mother (or sweetheart or wife, same thing).

In the end Miller turns to Foucault's question, What matter who's speaking? I agree with Miller that it matters very much who is speaking. Until the human mother speaks to her child and sees her/him as human *like herself*, nothing human has taken place and mattered. I agree with Miller that it is important to retain "the stability of the subject" which in my eyes can be none other than the mother. I think Miller is unlikely to concur with either of these suggestions. Certainly I concur with Miller slightly paraphrased: that in place of heroines in fiction "we might wish for instead . . . a female materialism attentive to the needs of the *[mother's]* body as well as the luxuries of the *[her]* mind.

7

The letters exchanged in 1989 between Peggy Kamuf and Nancy K. Miller are utterly delightful. As Miller says in her first letter to Kamuf, ". . . authorship is still a matter that engages us and locates us differently in the field of literary theory in which we both work. Whether this constitutes a 'conflict in feminism' is perhaps what this exchange will decide." It doesn't. Of course neither has in mind any connection between author and mother (or between authorship and motherhood) but that does not keep me from doing my own deconstructive reading, making these substitutions with, in my view, splendid results. Foucault, Derrida, and all anti-essentialists notwithstanding, the identity of the voice whether writing or speaking is most important; s/he as *functioning person* is the referent and signifier, not as is often claimed the text or the "content" of what is written or said. Even the "sign" of a footprint in the sand signifies nothing except that the entity whose impression it is has been actually, actively present at that location at some moment in time. As a sign, smoke signifies that fire is actively present at that given moment in time. As a sign, an infant signifies that a mother is actively present or nearby, or has only recently departed. Although every mother is a sign of a precedent mother, the one given to us in *our* time represents reality itself, the reality of Nature with a capital N: its temporality, its materiality, its actuality, and (in our case) its biological existentiality and social conventionality. Feminists too often ignore the fact that conventional social connections are but elaborations and extensions of physical connections, language being of far lesser import than the real presence of bodies. For the human species, our mother's body functions as our humanity and our intelligence; she is our social guide and our domestic stay. She alone is our authority and reference on all things that matter. Most certainly, she is the only possible universal referent for measuring the accuracy of theoretical hypotheses regarding feminism.

No doubt these assertions would horrify Miller and Kamuf and perhaps most academic feminists, but I believe most mothers will perceive the truth of what I am describing. Not incidentally, for I consider such data germane to conflicts in feminism, I'm quite eager to learn how many of the contributors to *Conflicts in Feminism* are functioning mothers. I sometimes consider counting women living with husbands or lovers among functioning mothers, since I see such commitments as a sexual act resembling motherhood. However, pregnancy (the carrying) and *caring* are to be distinguished from parturition. The moment a female embraces a male sexually, she is accepting the presence of and taking on the companionship of her "firstborn" so to speak. Notable, too, is the fact that males have no *way* to embrace females sexually, either figuratively or physically. The embrace belongs to our mother; within her arms, legs, and body *we* is bracketed.

In the letters, Miller observes that "The blindness of a feminist 'we' to its own exclusions has continued to complicate and deeply trouble the relations within feminism.... I'm thinking in particular of the powerful fiction of universal female subject.... This is not to say that I think 'we' should give up on feminism, or *its institutionalization as a project for cultural and social change....*" (My emphasis.) From my view, Miller then inadvertently reveals the inadequacy of her nonessentialist feminist epistemology in lamenting, "Where we are to go *from here*, and *in what language* ... is a lot less clear." (Her emphasis.) The tediousness of Kamuf's response sounds like Kristevan Lacanianism to me. Her response definitely reflects conventional male epistemology, which says that human knowledge derives from a male efficacy coming into the female system from "outside." Such male efficacy depends heavily upon language which is given the aura of "holy writ." From Kamuf's convoluted syntax, I gleaned the following to be what she is asking, or suggesting: If "there is no opposing opposition" means that "... there is ... no outside from which something else can intervene which is not already programmed by the dialectical machine, then one's oppositional strategy must fully espouse the logic of change ... made possible there and in those terms...." Using a good deal of deconstructivist jargon, she then asks something along the lines of, What if there are signs of opposition which could have come only from a space exceeding that structure? Such a sign "would signal its provenance by being non-opposable within the terms of that structure, that is, it would not fit simply on one side or the other of the line thought to divide the poles of the opposition...." "Put simply," she finishes, "I'm interested in the point at which a calculation ... according to a +/- binarism becomes impossible. In fact, I believe it's the only thing I find interesting." She reminds us that "there are no sealed-off cells." Kamuf says that if Miller is asking her to produce a *prescription* for a new politics beyond the oppositional logic Kamuf finds so inadequate, she will admit "I cannot do so.... However, does that demonstrate the irrelevance of any questions such as I and many others might want to pose to this 'oppositional logic'?"

These brilliant women simply do not see that it is man's theory of himself that requires an "oppositional logic." In it, woman is considered evil, a constant threat to man's attaining the godlike personage he *believes* (having been taught it is so) that he is foreordained to become. A feminist theory that uses the proper model of motherhood as the ultimate in becomingness has no necessity to mark man as threatening or evil. As in everything else so far touted, feminism is copying masculinism in insisting that man is the oppressor of woman, the bane of her existence. Kamuf writes to Miller concerning the "... question of what is or is not 'feminist' deserving the name ... if conflicts are all safely 'in' feminism, belong there together under the same title, if it is agreed in advance that that designation will gather all disagreements back into itself, then the outcome of these conflicts is predictable and contained." But, she puzzles, "... does feminism, *must* feminism sign itself 'return to sender unopened'?" (My emphasis.) I can answer

No. Motherhood's signature is "Please Forward." The space-time of the human mother's world of intelligent, practical imagination is endless; we have scarcely begun to explore and enjoy it. "There are no opposing oppositions" is a splendid rallying cry for feminists to adopt, especially Lesbian feminists, who I trust may come to see that male members are embraceable and quite useful, and in any case an inextricable property of the female body. Certainly it is understandable that mothers cherish their sons as valuable property and send them forth not to enrich themselves or to oppress their sisters but to return home with riches for the mothers and sisters to put to community use. That, after all, is the implied promise of a marital commitment between two "free" persons of different gender seeking to live in amity with one another. It is not unknown or unexperimented with for mothers to delegate authority at home and elect to range far and wide herself, gathering her own riches of experience and new ideas.

However specific social conventions are worked out, it is from the womb, the world and place of motherhood, that our life begins and continues to transpire. That is my answer to Miller's question, "From what place?" The inept, unguided (except by "deconstruction" and literary criticism) attempts of these two feminist authors, both professors and widely-sought lecturers, to pinpoint "positional distinctions" with respect to feminist "theory" flounder in the end for lack of a suitable *physical* model each might be expected to refer to. They seem to have nothing in mind except more words, more metaphors, more questions, and possibly just more opportunities to outrank or outflank feminist colleagues. Competitiveness of this type among a general population advocating and *practicing* essentialism as a premise of female commonality would be hard to imagine.

8

The title of Joan W. Scott's article is so offputting from my viewpoint that I almost skipped it: "Deconstructing Equality-Versus-Difference: Or, the Uses of Poststructuralist Theory for Feminism." That's quite a mouthful. What *objects*, what *physical model* can such a title possibly allude to? Scott is Professor of Social Science at *The* Institute for Advanced Study (my emphasis; the reader may already have surmised that in my opinion *the* institute for advanced *learning* is motherhood; how telling it is that academic feminists balk at citing motherhood as the entity which *any feminist theorizing* must focus on). In my view, *motherhood* needs theory, but that's not the way Scott nor many others see feminism. "In my own case," she writes, ". . . it was reading poststructuralist theory and *arguing with literary scholars* that provided the elements of clarification for which I was looking." (My emphasis.)

I read bravely on, and picked up the information that in poststructuralism Scott found ". . . a new way of analyzing constructions of meanings and relationships of power that called unitary, universal categories into question and historicized concepts otherwise treated as natural (such as man/woman) or absolute (such as equality or justice) . . . what attracted me was the historical connection between . . . Poststructuralism [sometimes she capitalizes it and sometimes she doesn't] and contemporary feminism . . . that share[s] a certain self-conscious critical relationship to established philosophical and political traditions. It thus seemed worthwhile for feminist *scholars* to *exploit* that relationship for *their* own ends." (My emphasis.)

I say, Good Luck. But before moving on, I would point out to these scholars that mothers are not "constructions of meaning" but rather the means by which and according to which we exist and enjoy our being in time. I admit that I do not understand the term "relationships of power." The physical connection that I observe between mothers and their offspring is one of the mother's authorship and determination, and the offsprings' compliance with her mode of existence. There are many powerful forces at work in Nature and motherhood is surely one of them. However, relative to her offspring, the human mother functions as physical model and social authority; "powerful" as in "coercive force" does not apply to her physiology, methodology, intent, or self-image (her understanding of her Self). The mother's dedicated intellectual and physical energy flows into the child; the efficacy of influence is something feminism can definitely count on, not "power."

9

Martha Minow's "Adjudicating Differences: Conflicts Among Feminist Lawyers" presents pro and con arguments for maternity leave as a "right" and pornography as a "right." The former has brought forward intense and somewhat unexpected discussions of gender and social equalities and inequalities seen as implicit in gender or artificially contrived by males, perhaps for the purpose of privileging the male gender. It has turned out that the right to produce and distribute pornography cannot be compromised under the U.S. Constitution's first amendment protecting free speech. These complex discursive processes lead Minow into emphasizing the law's reliance upon cultural conventions regarding private and public space and the notion that our private lives are distinct and separate from our public lives. Minow is a Professor of Law at Harvard Law School. Her article makes evident the overriding authority of both constitutional law and other codified laws governing every aspect of our cultural conventions. She points out that "law and public authority control the very definition of the family. Law determines what counts as a contract or a property right." She asserts that "Private actors may comply with or resist legal rules and thereby challenge law's claims to have the ultimate authority." (She does not mention the fact that on a per capita basis we have more transgressors of the law punitively incarcerated than any other country in the world.)

Minow asks what, to me, is one of the most interesting questions posed anywhere: What would happen if feminists resisted the framework of the public/private distinction altogether? Although I found her extenuating remarks and recommendations disappointing, her question, like all good questions, inspires a multitude of imaginative possibilities. Minow quotes Jean Bethke Elshtain's argument that each woman, like Antigone, is "excluded from legitimate statecraft unless she inherited a throne" and yet woman is "an active historic agent, a participant in social life who located the heart of her identity in a world bounded by the demands of necessity, sustaining the values of life-giving and preserving." Minow offers the suggestion that "One way to avoid the public/private debate might be to organize private boycotts of merchandisers who participate in the production, sale, or distribution of pornography . . . a boycott can remake the boundaries between public and private rather than line up competing political factions around the imagined divide between the two realms." She says that "Consciousness-raising and boycotts are less direct and obvious but potentially more effective and enduring methods for change than the actual creation of a new administrative scheme."

There are so many terms in these quotes that need clarifying that it is difficult to agree or disagree or even to be sure how Minow herself is reasoning. For instance, if the line between private and public is only imaginary (as I would agree that it is, and a *moralistic* imaginary line at that) why employ a strategy to "remake the boundaries?" To remake the boundaries of morality itself? That is one possible interpretation. But don't feminists need to work on the boundaries of female and male *identity* before we get involved in moral or private/public boundaries? "Actors" is a very unsatisfactory term if one is trying to figure out exactly what we "actors" are sexually doing besides entertaining each other or giving each other trouble. To me, *these questions are all connected and converge in any serious discussion of essentialism.* And what about arguments that usually rage over *legitimate* statecraft? To inherit a throne is to inherit the authority and presumably the responsibilities of a sovereign; new administrative schemes are surely something any sovereign may implement forthwith.

I would argue that as sovereign, the mother is only and forever our species' active agent for change. What the human mother has not yet learned is that although she correctly sees the child as herself, the child does not see her/himself as the mother. This is purely a matter of teaching. Since man's mastery of writing and publishing, it has been taught and preached not that we are made in the image of our mother but that we are made rather in the image of a male deity who loves us like *a father* loves *his son.* The mother is historic but history is rather a male obsession and academic woman's obsession with seeing herself "historically" is but another example of how woman has learned (also through man's mischievous misteachings) to see herself through men's eyes. The unschooled intelligent mother sees herself as a participant in Nature. This most intimate participation takes the form of a fate or calling indicative of the high privilege of being chosen or "ordained' and not the form of a "history" that could have gone one way or another as a result of something called "free will" or "self-determination." I argue in several other places in my response to *Conflicts in Feminism* that woman is sovereign over man as a result of her parturition and since the mother produces her own constituency, in effect she is the ship of state, the spacecraft in which we abide as we move through endless time.

Minow concludes with wise advice but few clues on how to implement such wisdom: "If feminists seek to challenge institutions that were designed without women in mind, and social practices that subordinate women, the construction of a feminist agenda must address all women.... As we struggle for new ways to struggle, we may begin to remake whom we mean by 'we', and thus transform our most critical tool: ourselves."

Here I can only repeat as forcefully as I can what I have said many times before in many other places:

1. Motherhood is the human institution around which we must rally and feminists need first to stop challenging motherhood as an institution that is here to stay; to challenge motherhood is to put oneself squarely in the camp of those who champion fatherhood as an institution.

2. Social practices are in the hands of every mother from the first hour of her parturition; it is impossible for any child whatever its gender to make the mother subordinate to the child in space, time, function, importance, or significance. The mother always *comes* first and she *stays* first.

3. By "we" the mother *always* means herself and her constituent offspring which she correctly views as a singularity, the singularity of her own body and maternal functions.

As for the agenda of mothers (I think it the same for every mother) and our struggles to achieve it, it couldn't be clearer or freer from hidden intents: *We* will make it *together.* For every sovereign mother, *we* is herself and her children. Mothers intend to make it *with their sons and daughters.* And so we shall, for Nature sees to it. The integrity and social health of every species depends upon the integrity (togetherness) and health of its offspring-bearing females. How or whether a confederacy of sovereign mothers could work out a global government for the species womankind is a very large question indeed. Whether or not sons intend to make it with their mothers/wives is an open question; what man's agenda is for the species is far from clear; man appears to have had only himself and his egocentric values in mind.

I consider it beyond dispute or discussion that the first step for feminists, if any there be, is to acknowledge the essentialism of motherhood and the pluralistic nature of authority. Feminism needs and must decide upon a *doctrine,* a *teaching,* and *the pluralistic authority of mothers* is it. This doctrine must and can hold sway against the monolithic "authority" of a thoroughly ridiculable male deity. Each mother is social arbiter and sovereign over the *public* lives of her children. The parturition of mothers introduces us to public space. The public arena always reflects home practices and home practices always reflect the mother's exertion of her own authority, which has nothing whatsoever to do with man's codified law, however "historical" that may be. How far each mother's jurisdiction extends as it encompasses community space and the sovereignty of other mothers and other constituencies is the fascinating task for feminists to work out. Nature is in charge of the private lives and destinies of all species. Scientific knowledge can help womankind a little, but in the final analysis, we have only probabilistic chances for survival. I find this not too upsetting, for my religious fidelity attaches to the principle of motherhood and the female as Nature's faithful, in essence immutable, agent.

10

As a philosopher, Helen E. Longino wants to ask "what the real philosophical differences are" as she discusses her own interests and positions with respect to feminism and those of Anne Fausto-Sterling, Evelyn Fox Keller, Donna Haraway, and Sandra Harding. In the same article, Evelynn Hammonds addresses "The Matter of Women *in* Science." Longino teaches philosophy at Rice University. Hammond is a physicist and a doctoral candidate in the History of Science at Harvard. Longino is an epistemologist and for my response to her I used both her article in *Conflicts in Feminism* (CF) and her paper in the November 1991 issue of *The Journal of Philosophy* (JP) entitled "Multiplying Subjects and the Diffusion of Power."

In the CF article, Longino says that "... we might anticipate deep and interesting metaphysical and epistemological differences.... When we look for explicit arguments ... and discount for rhetoric aimed at certain audiences, these anticipations turn to dust." She tells us that "... by an epistemological theory we mean a justificatory theory. Instead, we find recipes for inquiry, suggested procedures for deciphering Nature, none of which amount to *criteria for justification.*" (My emphasis.) Her best questions in my view are, "What are the consequences of directing our philosophical attention away from propositional knowledge to the relationship between scientist and phenomena" and "Why do we persist in framing our arguments within the traditional categories, thus magnifying our differences?" What no epistemologist, including Longino, seems ever to think to consider is that human knowledge depends *first* upon cognition of our *sexual functions. Historically,* these have been amazingly transformed by the feats of *propositional* "knowledge" *while the functions themselves have remained quite untransformed.*

In her conclusion of the JP article, Longino interestingly says that the "... need for models within which we can situate ourselves and the interactions we desire with the natural world *will militate against* the inclusiveness required for an adequate critical practice ..." (My emphasis.) Her reason is that "... inclusion of the less powerful ... will always be a matter of conflict." She speaks of "the demand for inclusiveness" of the "politically marginal" and expresses uneasiness about conflation of the marginal with the crackpot. It seems safe to assume that epistemologists no less than theologians and scientists keep a good portion of their cognitive powers focused silently on their sexuality, for that is what daily life comprises.

The traditional categories will always be female and male. And in my book the knowing subject will always be the mother and the object known will always be the child. The child and not the mother is the inquirer; she reasons but does not inquire out of *curiosity* to know more than she already lamentably knows. She knows Nature firsthand, and all about Nature's carelessness; she is Nature's knowing victim but her knowledge does not make her free. As knowing subject, the human mother must find quietening if not jolly answers to her child's questions; it would never do to tell her/him the murderous facts of life and the futility of it all. Mothers love it when sons and spouses "do" science, enter the church, and otherwise distinguish themselves by their studies.

Longino's bottom line is that "*. . . the structures of cognitive authority themselves must change. No segment of the community, whether powerful or powerless, can claim epistemic privilege.*" (JP, my emphasis.) It seems evident to me that the human mother's segment of the community *can and must* claim epistemic privilege. Motherhood comprises the very structure of cognitive authority in the human case. Would-be epistemologists must *first answer* the most basic of all questions concerning human knowledge: Are the questions "What can woman know and how can she know it?" *different* from the questions "What can man know and how can he know it?" In short, *can woman and man be conflated into one being, manifesting one body of knowledge*? Obviously, the answer must be yes, in view of two indisputable facts: that man is borne son of woman and that she *keeps him* as her true spouse. But this is to ignore *propositional truth and logic* which themselves are inventions of man and favorites of all theologians and scientists.

All propositions begin with a given. Given god, man has argued for eons that although he comes *through* woman he is not essentially *of* her body or being, not part *of* her cognitive, carnal self-knowledge. Hordes of human beings traipse to mosque, synagogue, and church to reaffirm every week, every day, and every hour the proposition that man himself comes from god and that he must *keep himself* close to god. The closer one is to god the more distant one is from any taint of female sexuality. So much for propositional truth and logic as applied to self-knowledge.

Significantly, so-called "scientific" knowledge does not include self-knowledge, Freud notwithstanding. Supposedly, scientific knowledge is neutral, that is, genderless. And now, according to Longino, *woman* must strive for a *neutral* place in which to do science *with men*. The crucial point which epistemologists and most especially *feminists* ignore is that man's attitude towards woman is *never* neutral, nor is woman's towards man, her very own systemically produced son and spouse.

There is no shortage of accounts of how and why scientific knowledge is constantly changing, being modified and adjusted by scientists to accommodate "new findings." These ever new data are supposed to relate to and be applicable to material objects. But the material objects proceed merrily on their way, unaffected by what we say or think about them. Science as told by scientists is truly a story, carefully plotted for rapt consumption by a believing community. It's a great honor, for instance, to be invited to tell a story before a gathering of the members of the American Philosophical Association. But one must be prepared to defend the credibility of one's tale: why is it worthy in all seriousness to be believed?

How does *the speaker* know that what *the speaker* is telling us is true? Why should the speaker care about truth so long as we believe and *follow*? This is where "knowledge" magically becomes power. What keeps any story from being the hallucination of a crackpot and what matter that, so long as the constituent community believes and *follows*? Acquiring scientific knowledge unrelated to self-knowledge is the most glorious way in the world to escape the pain and glare of existential truth. No wonder woman wants a piece of the scientific pie. It's certainly the case that children, men, and scientists seem to be having all the fun at the expense of women and mothers.

If there is to be a feminist epistemology, the justification for what *mothers* know must point squarely to *how* we know it, and this is to point to the essentialism of woman's parturition, which has nothing to do with language. The mother is a nonpropositional given. We know when we are mothers by *doing* what mothers do; some but not all mothers *understand* what that "do-ty" comprises and entails. Essentialism works either way, whether we interpret or misinterpret what we do. Essentialism has to do with the actual physical, biological, dynamic efficacy of motherhood however it is described, falsely described, understood, or misunderstood.

Philip Kitcher's response to Longino's JP article points out that "scientific knowledge is a social achievement. Individual knowers are epistemically dependent on those around them." This is not true of the mother's knowledge of her own parturition, which is as empirical as knowledge can get. I answer a reluctant *Yes* to Longino's final question (in CF): ". . . could it be that our construction of . . . differences is itself refracted through the father's eye, through *his* language, *his* questions, for *his* attention?" (Longino's emphasis.) Present day *society's* construction of "differences" is definitely a male construction. I do not include myself in the above "our," but maybe that is why I write for an audience that seems at times to be no more than one, yet this I am unwilling to accept lying down.

Clearly, I am not in agreement with academic epistemologists nor they with me. Nevertheless, or possibly all the more, I am convinced that the majority of human mothers will understand well enough what I am trying to say, and will be inclined to agree. I write for mothers who understand their own sexuality and its all-encompassing social function. I hope there are increasing numbers of professors to be found among this group.

Evelynn Hammond in a few words makes the case that ". . . we have yet to demonstrate *how* the scientific method can provide successful representations of the physical world while at the same time inscribing social structures of domination and control in its institutional, conceptual, and methodological core." (My emphasis.) In itself, this is a curiously constructed sentence, but the answer to the *how* seems evident. Science provides "successful representations of the physical world" by *inscription,* and it is also through inscription that man manipulates social structures of domination and control: scientific equations and holy writ have much in common. Scientists and theologians have prudently stayed out of each others' territory. Science has never focused on applying its knowledge to the ordering of human cultures; religion has focused on doing exactly that.

Now that women have breached both territories, I believe that both scientific and religious versions of "reality" will be greatly altered *descriptively,* that is, so far as *inscription* and annotations of what is significant goes. But this has always been the case: everyone sees things differently and describes things differently and given the chance, structures things differently. The most that can be hoped is that females *in general* think more pragmatically and more in terms of serving the human community, and that we are not so vainglorious in our ambitions. And it seems to me that this can be hoped most confidently *when the women are also mothers.*

It seems next to impossible for men to move from childhood to adulthood since they habitually and naturally surround themselves with female "support staff." It also seems next to impossible for women and especially mothers not to settle for supportive roles all their lives long. Mothers are our natural authority figures. A mother's voice is certainly a different voice from the father's voice. The point is that every father's voice is the voice of a son, a child's voice, triumphant in his determined domination of the mother, utterly convinced that he, the child, knows best what is best for the mother. Why are mothers so reluctant to call the child's bluff? Why do we *expect* to be permissive, adoring parents and, failing to discipline and to *teach,* expect not to have to face horrible throwbacks to animalistic behavior and worse in our daughters and sons? The price of civilization is the constant vigilance of mothers in private and public domains where *sexuality* is as always the sovereign good.

How the mother structures social norms concerning the approach to and use of her own body, how she alone structures the dispensing of the largesse of her own person, she alone must decide. The son and the father will not listen gladly but they will conform, for indeed they must. The daughter as usual will find herself on her own, setting her own standards for the conduct of her own constituent children and her lovers, who are but sons of some other mother.

11

Taking the form of a question, "Race, Class, and Psychoanalysis?", Elizabeth Abel's essay gives her reading of "two dense and brilliant texts that address the intersections of gender with race or class from perspectives both indebted to and critical of psychoanalysis." The texts are Hortense J. Spillers' "Mamma's Baby, Papa's Maybe: An American Grammar Book," and Carolyn Kay Steedman's "Landscape for a Good Woman: A Story of Two Lives." Spillers works primarily with Lacan, and Steedman primarily with object relations, according to Abel. She says that "each asserts and subverts a range of psychoanalytic and social discourses and propels them into provocative and complicated play." Since the term "race" signifying color and the term "class" signifying poverty or economic wealth are incomprehensible to me as in any way applicable to gender or to feminist theory, I found the extraordinarily "complicated play" extraordinarily unedifying. By arousing the greatest possible emotion, the stories Abel relays to us dwell on what is of least interest to the main question, which is, in my view, how to understand and accurately describe the dynamic connection between the mother as female subject and her offspring. In other words, how does the two-gendered biological system work in the human case? We must figure out with some accuracy the special features of our biological system, which attaches to itself an extraordinary language originating in the mother's tongue, before we can figure out how our social conventions take the forms they do.

Many feminists have adopted psychoanalysis as an appropriate tool for delving into psychic phenomena and emotional experiences of women. These feminists are convinced, presumably, that psychoanalysis is a science of human development with some predictive capabilities. As such, its theory, based on certain hypotheses concerning the human psyche and our conscious and unconscious sexual drives, is something these feminists must find acceptable. Talking about one's early childhood experiences and about one's dreams is supposed to reveal all the wrong turns and regrettable encounters that brought on all the physical anguish and mental disorders with which the speaker can no longer cope. If the discourse is addressed to a competent analyst, all kinks and quirks eventually may be straightened out and after the analyst gives his (or her) final blessing and dismissal, the loquacious one may go forth in peace to err no more. I don't buy it. Scientific method: principles and procedures for the systematic pursuit of knowledge involving the recognition and formulation of a problem; the collection of data through observation and experiment, and the formulation and testing of hypotheses (Webster's New Collegiate Dictionary). The problem of course is dysfunction. Psychic dysfunction is intimately tied to sexual dysfunction and probably vice versa. In our species, what is the measure for properly functioning sexual health? I argue that the mother's sexuality is the only possible standard by which to take the measure of our species, in sickness or in health. Women and mothers are now so sexually sick which is to say dysfunctional that we can hardly remember or imagine ourselves sexually healthy. I believe that only a feminist psychoanalytic theory of motherhood can pull us out of this quagmire of sexual confusion.

In her concluding paragraph, Abel says "It is too early for feminism to foreclose on psychoanalysis. . . . Psychoanalysis has been resistant to the social, but it need not always, uniformly, be. It is better for feminism to challenge that resistance than to renounce psychoanalysis entirely or succumb to its seductions." My quarrel is not with psychoanalysis but with Freud's masculinism. While the social and the sexual are undeniably intertwined, and the intricate discourses on sexuality that Spillers and Steedman recount and deconstruct contain most sorrowful *social* factors such as racism, poverty, slavery, exploitation, ignorance, and degradation, among others, nowhere do these feminists offer suggestions of how our sexual system as a *system* is *theoretically* supposed to work. I would hope that a feminist deconstruction of psychoanalysis might make clear that race and class are irrelevant to the dynamics of our sexual system. True, object relations sets up a paradigm of the attachment of infants to their mothers which to feminists like Nancy Chodorow seems a sound enough basis from which to hypothesize an original feminist theory. However, object relations' hypothesis that gender differences originate in infantile developmental processes seems preposterous, as does the notion *as an hypothesis* that female and male infants exhibit different "struggles" to "separate from the mother." As I see our species' overarching existential system, the social order is but an extension of the mother's biological system. However much we may "struggle" to distance ourselves from particular mothers, we cannot separate from the system. It seems to me that such a term as "struggle," like the delusional distancing and all sorts of talk about alienation, separation, the establishment of autonomy and so forth, derives from false notions of how the human sexual system works. I view the male as remaining attached to the mother, who is the system, all his life long. The female also remains attached to the mother, extending the system in space-time and allowing the male members to cling to her even as her mother did.

Lacan himself says that, "The relation of the subject to the Other is entirely produced in a process of gap." In a feminist theory of psychoanalysis, I think the correct referent for this process and this gap is the mother's parturition where one becomes two in space-time. Girls mature, have babies, and proceed to extend the continuum in space-time of our species' system. This procedure of female sexual functions ultimately provides intelligent human mothers with absolute certain knowledge of the facts of life. Man's mature sexual function provides him only with the means to stay connected to the female system and to remain a functioning part of its sexual dynamic. Man's experience of the facts of life is very limited compared with the mother's. His is more comparable to the child's experience; both are forced by their appetitive need for the mother to sensibly cling to her system. The sensibilities of the body cannot be discounted or ignored by intellections presumed to be more sensible and usually, or so the reasoning goes, more protective of self. These conflicts and quandaries are the stock in trade of psychoanalysis but Freud has so badly mislabeled the items and so poorly understood how they go together to make a dynamic, workable system, that feminism would do well to turn elsewhere for descriptive terms and explanations of dynamic connections.

Motherhood as a system and mothering as a practice separate biology from social conventions. The sociologist Chodorow's reproduction of mothering "theory" attempts to address some of the social aspects of our mothering practices. Nowhere does it get to the heart of motherhood as the essential system any genuine feminist theory must first understand and then use to elucidate the desire and need of all of us offspring for the mother. The Other is an ambiguous, ill-understood and ill-used term in psychoanalysis as well as in theologies. Among members of a consanguine, healthy species, there is no alien Other. No mortal enmity among members is thinkable, expressible, or possible. A member or property that is integral to a system's dynamic function cannot be alienated *by the system* from which it evolved and where it found an harmonious and useful place. The toughest and most awesome question to ask is, *Is it possible* for a member or property that was once harmoniously integrated within a system to turn cancerous, setting itself up to feast off of the system until the system itself is dead and buried, without a thought or care concerning its own treachery and self-defeating pleasures?

Lacan has written that "... psychoanalysis might be reduced to the rank of something with whose forms and history it so often suggests an analogy—namely, a church and, therefore, a religion." If so, I would insist that it must be the religion or institution of motherhood in contradistinction to the religion or institution of fatherhood. "But," says Lacan, "psychoanalysis is not a religion. It proceeds from the same status as

Science.... It is engaged in the central lack in which the [male] subject experiences himself as desire." Here I would interject that the mother, as female subject, experiences herself as the desirable. Woman has not the same passion to know that man has, and that is because in parturition she gains a certain knowledge of herself and a certain understanding of her function that man has no way of gaining. Lacan is splendid when he correctly lumps together the passion of philosophers (Descartes in particular), the religious in general, and scientists in general to know something beyond doubt, to know with absolute certainty. He also with great forthrightness and honesty equates such "certain knowledge" with belief: scientists and secularized psychoanalysts, no different from religious believers, fall back upon faith in "a knowing subject," an ultimate authority whose word or principle is law. In Descartes' case, the ultimate knowing subject is god; in the case of scientists and psychoanalysts, it is the principles of Nature as understood and interpreted by *men*. If, like Lacan, one equates the analyst with the ultimate "knowing subject," one must also assume Descartes' male god to be *man's* ultimate knowing subject. Sure enough, male analysts do so assume, or keep very quiet about any disagreement with Judaic beliefs, shoring up all of their uncertainties with the certainty that god gave man dominion over woman and Nature.

There is much in Lacan that can be drawn on to help feminists hammer out a genuine pschoanalytical theory that accurately reflects the existential processes that take place in space-time. For instance, refuting his claim that "Psychoanalysis touches on sexuality only inasmuch as . . . it manifests itself in the defile of the signifier, in which is constituted the dialectic of the subject in the double stage of alienation and separation. Analysis has not kept, on the field of sexuality, what one might, mistakenly, have expected of it by way of promises—it has not kept such promises because it does not have to keep them. This is not its terrain." As I have earlier indicated, the terrain of psychoanalysis is social practice, helping dysfunctional individuals to conform to a "normal" social praxis that is predetermined by the knowledgeable analyst to be desirable, at least from his or her viewpoint. Freud has been faulted for presuming his very Jewish viewpoint to be universal. Whether or not it is desirable has not been questioned. Men obviously desire it as a viewpoint. Feminists, female and male, must institute a materialistic unidealized essentialist theory of motherhood in its place for the sake of physical accuracy. Whether or not essentialism is desirable as a theory is a moot question. Theory that gets it right has no choice but to let the fur fly.

Lacan's viewpoint is hidden under the odd notion that the symbolic is the real, an idea that turns out to be thoroughly congenial with monotheistic male-oriented religions. Always straightforward, Lacan said in a famous seminar: "... I ask the question—*What are the fundamentals,* in the broad sense of the term, *of psychoanalysis?* Which amounts to saying—What grounds it as praxis? ... What is a praxis? ... It is the broadest term to designate a concerted human action, whatever it may be, which places man in a position to treat the real by the symbolic." (Lacan's emphasis.) I honestly believe that such self-serving nonsense must not be taken seriously by serious feminists. What we must take seriously is motherhood as the system all fields of knowledge must relate their knowledge to. The child is not symbolic. Man is not symbolic. Religious symbols signify nothing but cherished beliefs. Nothing in the mother's reality is symbolic. All of our female functions are real happenings that must be clearly described in their systemic, dynamic wholeness before we start thinking, remembering, or discussing how it was with us as individuals.

It will take many papers and books and perhaps generations before feminists reach some consensus concerning the systemic, dynamic wholeness of our sexual female functions A good beginning I think would be to agree that the female is an attractant, a magnetic force, a desirable object. Things are drawn to us and we aggrandize everything that is unto ourselves. The female is a dynamic system of specially energized space, possessing the amazing capability of continuing its unique form and identity in space-time, adjusting and accommodating itself to whatever random encounters come along in space-time to be aggrandized and used, discarded, or avoided. I doubt not that in the universe there are always an infinity of female systems avoiding nothing, for they are ever inclined by Nature to find a use for everything. Nature, surely, is being served by this method. As an energized female system, does the human mother desire to be what she is, or would she rather be spared the driving necessity to perform her female functions? Does performing her female functions bring her any pleasure, or is she rather bored by the routine of it all? If she sees that she has no choice, that reproduction is a futile treadmill, what inspires her energy, why doesn't it dissipate, grow quiet, and her system disappear into the undifferentiated chaos of space-time? If all the things that are deliciously drawn to her to take their pleasure in tapping into her system and to sate their desire, is she necessarily desireless, so sated is she? To me, it seems at least possible that in the cognitive (human) case, our mother's desire is the perceived pleasure of satisfying the desires of others, of giving others life (her own). If so, is there an attractant, a force to which the female finds herself drawn, to which she desires to attach herself and so to be at last granted her fulfillment of a passionate longing which intermittently has been denied? I believe the answer to this question is Yes, that for dynamically whole females the attractant is Nature and that woman's passion to serve Nature in health and wholeness is intelligence itself.

Ending this too-long response to Elizabeth Abel's invocation of objects relations as a theory of human relationships and Lacan psychoanalytical constructs, I will quote Lacan on desire: "... You see, the object of desire is the cause of the desire, and this object that is the cause of desire is the object of the drive—that is to say, the object around which the drive turns. ... It is not that desire clings to the object of the drive—desire moves around it, insofar as it is agitated in the drive. But all desire is not necessarily agitated in the drive. There are empty desires or mad desires that are based on nothing more than the fact that *the thing in question has been forbidden you.* By virtue of the very fact that it has been forbidden you, you cannot do otherwise, for a time, than think about it. That, too, is desire. But whenever you are dealing with *a good object*, we designate it—it's a question of terminology, but a justified terminology—as an object of love." (Emphasis added.)

If it is true that in the human case the intelligent female no longer is attracted by Nature to function as a mother, what now is woman's mad desire? Is it a fact that woman has the option to thwart Nature, or is such a thought but an indication of inferior intellect, of thinking like a man in supposing some good god science has bestowed on her such powers of self-determination?

12

Thomas W. Laqueur's article, "The Facts of Fatherhood," is not to be believed. It is a transparent rationalization of man's overpowering passion to be parent of woman's child. The way I see it, since man cannot pull off the most desirable situation, which would be to displace the mother altogether, as "father" he jealously "shares" parenthood with the entity who bears "his" offspring but who in fact bore and bears the "father." The nearer man can come to tarring woman as a nonentity, the more he preens himself on being mother in her place. In the priesthood this is the ceremony of being ordained a "father-in-god." This ritual represents a thoroughgoing *historic* male deconstruction of the entirely factual "mother-in-goodness" who produces sons, many of whom (but far from all) become overly ambitious fathers. This is not the way Laqueur sees things, needless to say.

Using the case of Baby M as one example among others, Laqueur recounts the law's interpretation of how conventional and unconventional "fatherhood" works. "What exactly are the facts of motherhood and what of significance ought to follow from them?" he asks but does not answer. He cites examples of how the law works to concede a *vested* interest of the father in "his" child. The mother invests little more than her labor, Laqueur claims, and he is quick to point out that "Capitalist societies . . . are not usually friendly to the notion that putting labor into a product entitles one to ownership or even to much credit. . . . Having the *idea* or the *plan* is what counts." Which is why, he says, the Judge told a father that in accordance with the law, which in this Judge's hands gave the child to the father instead of to the surrogate mother, the father was "only getting what was already his." And Laqueur actually adds magnanimously, in parentheses, "(The Judge should, of course, have said, 'half his'.)."

Laqueur confesses to having become exercised over the case of Baby M "because Dr. Stern's claims have been reduced in some circles to his ownership of his sperm which . . . amounts to owning very little." He goes on to acknowledge that all fathers are "at a distinct material disadvantage to . . . all women . . . who contribute so much more matter." He then resorts to a sentimental argument that the "father's" claims to the child, no different from the mother's, "arise from the intense and profound bonding with a child, unborn and born, that its biological kinship might spark in the moral and affective imagination but which it does not entail." Conceding that the mother's biological kinship with her child doesn't necessarily spark a moral and affective imagination in many mothers, perhaps a majority of mothers, doesn't help Laqueur's case. There's no evidence that a preponderance of "fathers" can be counted on to display moral and affective imagination as they bond with their children. Anyway, according to Laqueur it is because of this "emotional capital" and not any biological connection that a surrogate mother ". . . must be *allowed* a reasonable time to change her mind and if she does, in the case of a surrogacy arrangement, be prepared to *argue* for her *rights* against those of the father." (My emphasis.) Laqueur does not take up the matters of *who* does the allowing, and *who* determines the merits of her arguments or the extent of her *rights* in contradistinction to the father's *rights* for the possession and custody of the child, who is clearly a *property* of the mother. The child is not a commodity laboriously made by hand or by any labor-saving machine. The child evolved out of a physical system commonly described as female and intimately connected with Nature, the same physical system the male member is a dynamic part of, but the male member is not the source of the child's life, he is not parent.

Laqueur correctly sees the present social situation as both conflictual and dichotomous but he is wrong in seeing the dichotomy as irrelevant or the conflict as unresolvable by biological facts. "Each parent would bring to *such a battle* claims to have made another person emotionally part of themselves," he observes. His final conclusion seems an attempt to be fair: "While we can continue to look forward to continuing *conflict* over the *competing claims of parents*, I suggest that we abandon the notion that biology—facts—will somehow provide the resolution. Neither, of course will ideas alone.... The way out of the fact/idea dichotomy is to recognize its irrelevance in these matters. The 'facts' of such socially powerful and significant *categories as mother and father* come into being only as culture imbues things, actions, and flesh with meaning. This is the *process* that demands our continued attention." (My emphasis; his scare quotes on "facts.") I couldn't agree more. Social processes have been profoundly affected of late by influence from the "fathers": our male-dominated culture has imbued objects, actions, and flesh itself with values that seem increasingly questionable as to their meaning, or benefit to the species, I would add. Under mother-dominated cultures I believe things, actions, and flesh are imbued with decidedly more community-minded, more imaginative, and certainly less aberrated values. More to the point, the allegiance of children to the mother's singular authority must not be torn by claims of dichotomous parenthood. After all is said and done, the real function of fathers is to be lovers and supporters of the system that bears them. The most wonderful example a father can set for his children is a display of his own glad obedience to the mother. Let fathers focus their moral and affective imagination on keeping the mother's system strong. This of course requires fathers to give up their jealous passion to have *authority* over their own children. Once the authority of mothers is reestablished throughout all social institutions, the son and the father will get the message that the male member has *no* authority over mother, spouse, or child.

13

Sara Ruddick's excursis on birthgivers and the place of the father in family life seems an opaque example of the centrality of the father in the thinking of many self-declared feminists. The profusion and diffusion of *social* problems throughout human cultures is easily traceable to the dominance of males, without whom there is no two-gendered system. While eager to somehow rectify the dominance of males, feminists of Ruddick's ilk seem reluctant to examine the ever so much more dominant influence of the essentialist mother. Ruddick and others write as though the essentialism of motherhood is virtually inadmissible and not to be taken seriously in any feminist analysis of what humanity is supposed to be about. I would suggest that feminist writers who are into literature are not necessarily into *feminism* so long as they prefer literary figures (for example,Virginia Woolf and Hannah Arendt) as role models in place of their less glamorous mothers. It is extremely difficult to think about one's mother without thinking either *with* her or *against* her. Feminism, I suggest, will not have come into maturity as a philosophy, a therapy, and a political theory of governance by mothers until self-named feminists fully realize that thinking *with* one's mother, from her *place*, is the only prospectus that can with some accuracy forecast and map a salvific course for humanity.

The *biological* story cannot conceal the fact that, as Gertrude Stein didn't remark, children are burdensome. Sara Ruddick's article, "Thinking About Fathers," feebly strikes at responding to Laqueur's article but her response achieves no depth. She is well aware of "the official story" which places man in the home as lord and master. She asks, "If putative fathers are absent or perpetually disappearing and actual present fathers are controlling or abusive, who needs a father?" Ruddick describes "a Herland in which men as well as women would live safely because women would govern." She describes feminists who, rather than attempting to free mothers from men, "... work to transform the institutions of fatherhood. "Ruddick envisions "... a world where many more men are more capable of participating fully in the responsibilities and pleasures of mothering ..." She admits, "... I have only to open a newspaper ... to find myself fantasizing about a world without Fathers.... Because so many daughters, mothers, and wives have lived a sorry history of fatherhood, a feminist needs to imagine and justify her confidence in new ways of fathering. For this task, the words, as well as the work, of good and thoughtful fathers are indispensable.... Thomas Laqueur is a good father." But Laqueur, she points out with emphasis, "is not much interested in the analysis of domestic power."

Ruddick is a good example of the anti-essentialist feminist mentality that will use almost any term except "mother" or "motherhood" to indicate the function or category "mother." She uses the annoying term "birthgiver." She sees, I think correctly, that Laqueur "... sets up a contest between female birthgivers and male progenitors.... Laqueur tips the scales to the father by highlighting his emotional response to a genetic offspring and the birthgiver's insensitive or muddled reactions.... Laqueur ignores ... the birthgiver's response to the fetal-infant life she carries and delivers." After a few more flip-flops on the terms that signify which parent does what, Ruddick states her position and her question:

> In making the case for "mothering" as a gender-inclusive and therefore genderless activity, I have been struck by the resis-

> tance even of those men who fully engage in child-tending. As a feminist I am aware of the dangers of "saming" (to borrow a useful phrase from Naomi Schor) that is, denying the objectified other—in this case the male parent—"the right to [his] difference, submitting the other to the laws of [maternity]." *But I do not understand what men fear to lose. Leaving aside penis, sperm, . . . and other "essentialist" and essentially unthreatened equipment, what makes a parent a "father"?* (My emphasis.)

Later on, Ruddick strengthens her real point:

> Despite my refusal of the abstract "parent" and the different "father," I am as determined as Laqueur to disrupt the presumption that female birthgiving is either necessary or sufficient for good-enough mothering. I see all mothers, including women-mothers who have given birth, as "adoptive." A man or woman is a "mother," in my sense of the term, only if he or she acts upon *a social commitment to nurture, protect, and train children.* All mothering depends upon some woman's birthgiving but *there are many possible birth-respecting relationships between mothers and birthgivers.* (My emphasis.)

Then, she finally says it:

> Finally, however, my account of "adoptive" maternal work and thinking comes no closer than Laqueur's labor theory of parenting to articulating a social, political, and metaphysical *understanding of birth.* (My emphasis.)

As I have repeatedly said, how and what I *do* uncovers my identity of who I am; and it is the *socially instituted office of authority* that the Name of the Father has no intention of relinquishing to the *naturally instituted* and therefore more authentic and surely everlasting authority of the mother. The opportunity to experience parturition is not given to any male yet it is this experience alone that establishes the mother's sure knowledge of what she does and therefore who she is: the mother, the person who authors and issues forth new versions of herself. Ruddick and the literary crowd look upon this everyday experience as less than monumental, in fact, as too trivial to warrant serious discursive thought at all. They are into professional scholarship, academic careers, comparison of great women with the questionable greatness of men. I find these efforts of minimal interest or application to feminist theory. From the human mother's singular viewpoint, the mother astutely observes that it is her son who appears to be other than her whole self. However, she figures out that he is a vital member of her whole self with a function as specific as her heart, eyes, or ears. Like our opposable thumbs which first evolved out of some special beneficial use to the species, men are now put to so many uses and activities that generally benefit the species that their originary purpose is quite unimportant and almost forgotten. For many ages females have not thought of social or sexual encounters with males as being for the sole purpose of impregnation.

Most social functions are highly variant, and none more so than the use to which mothers put men in the construct of their family life. Most physical functions are quite invariant. Insemination is an invariant male function while gestation and parturition are invariable female functions. Feminism I think is, or should be, entirely about how females function first physically and then socially *as mothers*. But feminists like Ruddick want to be *more than just mothers* while men like Laqueur want to be *more than just inseminators*. Neither party seems wild about the idea of doing all the boring maintenance work that domestic life and childrearing demand. This shirking is part of the package of ignoring the significance of motherhood altogether. Shirking the tediousness of motherhood also leads to the establishment of a servant class, and classism leads to racism. Ruddick says that many feminists, "...and I among them, envision a world where many more men are more capable of participating fully in the responsibilities and pleasures of mothering...." Surely she is right in claiming that "...Any man or woman can assume the responsibilities and *share* in the pleasures of maternal work, whatever his or her relationship to the birthgivers of the children they tend...." (My emphasis.) Surely any community member *could* come to the aid of the helpless child once borne and born. But what mother can count on it? Feminism cannot be solely about such arguments and counter-arguments, nor is feminism about literary critiques, or treatments of disengaged "texts." *Motherhood* is the text, and the *context* of motherhood is the mother's parturition, during which act and function she confronts herself face to face. This is no mirror image of herself, nor an imaginary, fictive idealization of herself. The child is *simultaneously* the mother's past and future selves. There is no possible way that *the child* can comprehend his place or function in this overall reality the mother sees so clearly.

For too many feminists, reading novels appears to be a far far better thing to do than to contemplate the essentialism of one's own motherhood *in conjunction with* the motherhood of one's own mother and the inevitable motherhood of one's daughter. This brings up a point of motherhood and regeneration that is usually glossed over by mothers and would-be "fathers" alike: regeneration has to be counted from mother to mother, from parturition to parturition. Seeds do not represent regeneration. Regeneration can never be counted as from father to son, nor from mother to daughter. Until an offspring has proved itself fruitful, no extension of the species has transpired, no new generation has succeeded in renewing its kind. This is why the term "progenitor" is such a misnomer and why family trees showing the lineage of males is such a travesty of historical fact. Ruddick places herself in a direct *intellectual* line with Virginia Woolf and feminists are really into this sort of identity but I believe such efforts can be of little benefit to a hard-driving feminist philosophy based upon a sound theory of the essentialism of motherhood as instituted at the moment of parturition.

The business of renewing our kind is the exclusive business of mothers. It is also the business of mothers to exhibit what *kind* we are. It's pretty obvious that like all other species we are the kind that cares more for our offspring than we care for ourselves. In essence, this is the exemplary care of the *authentic* authority figure (the mother) holding an instituted office of authority (the office and institution of motherhood) caring more for the constituency (her children) than she does for herself. There is no public performance versus private activity. Mothers don't fatten themselves privately while watching their constituency starve, as do popes, kings, and heads of secular states. Your average human mother is not into goodness, beauty, or justice. But she finds herself forced by circumstances to deal pragmatically with starkest truth, incurable inequities, and the necessity of charity. The realization and actualization of the *essential facts of life* take place in parturition.

Ruddick has written about her own mother but far more extensively about Virginia Woolf's relation to her mother, noting that, "... If Woolf was in some sense a mother, she was even more a daughter who expressed daughterly longings and confusions remarkably like my own..." Ruddick apparently would like to encourage a commitment among feminists to a *discourse* based upon certain values and ways of seeing that she describes as "maternal thinking." Maternal thinking, according to Ruddick, is a result of bearing children, nursing infants, preserving and generally caring for life. Its pacifism distinguishes it from the thoughts of men, although the maternal way of thinking is available to men as well as to women who have not borne children. Plainly, this is a form of humanism and as such greatly dependent upon enlightened education. To me, the essentialism of motherhood and the epistemology of how and what the mother knows are of another dimension entirely. The mother can relay her social values to daughters and to sons, but it is unlikely they will be heeded by either. No one *speaks* to or for the new generation. The posit, the relay, must be made in *kind*. Dialectics is no substitute for parturition, the only means by which a species furthers its existence for better or for worse. Feminists need to rethink the logic of the female system whose complex reproduction of itself involves two genders, only one of whom does all the dynamic work the process requires. Thinking about fathers is secondary to the more urgent analysis of the son and his place in the social constructs that necessarily follow the phenomenon of parturition.

From my reading of Laqueur, and Ruddick's response, I see no signs that either perceives the envy, fear, resentment, and guilt that the son's disqualification for motherhood engenders in males. The task, as she sees it, "... is to construct—really *construct,* socially, materially, and politically—birthgiving practices in which women and men can participate unequally but with realistic self-respect, mutual regard, and a commitment to the well-being of the children that they, or other mothers, will adopt." She is wrong when she adds, "This is of course utopian." On the contrary, it's what we've got. Neither humanists nor feminists have been grounded enough in motherhood and the authentic authority of mothers to construct a state *publicly* run by mothers although everyone knows mothers are the kingmakers, the salt of the earth, and the essential figures, not to say servant class, upon which all societies depend. What feminists like Ruddick really seem to be saying is, *I want to be more than a servant. Intelligent* men sometimes conclude that they want to be *more than the one served* but even *very* intelligent men have balked at serving the servant. Habit is strong and nothing is more habit-forming than being a child. We never outgrow our longing for an *idealized* mother, of being the one graciously served and adored. Is every half-way contented mother playing a charade? Does she really hate it, wishing she were other places doing different things, for instance, reliving her own childhood, or possibly floating in the prenatal bliss of total custodial care, in that place where the ever-wonderful mother does it all?

14

I was inspired to give King-Kok Cheung's article a specially appreciative reading since the wife of one of my sons is Chinese and I have been watching their two children, my grandsons, grow up in a small West Coast town. Cheung's belief is that

". . . in order to understand conflicts among diverse groups of women, we must look at the relations between women and men, especially where the problems of race and gender are closely intertwined." However, she notes, ". . . Attempts at cultural reconstruction, whether in terms of 'manhood' and 'womanhood', or of 'mainstream' versus 'minority' heritage, are often inseparable from a wish for self-empowerment."

Since I believe that the *place* of the mother is quite universal, I also believe that, as a group, mothers are not as diverse as some suppose. In order to understand social *and personal* conflicts (the two seem inseparable), I look to the relations between wives and husbands, both of whom, it seems to me, look to parenthood as an appropriate arena for their own authoritative empowerment as primary parent. Parental conflicts, I have observed, are often traceable to the habit-forming relations that take place between mothers and sons from the moment of birth. In this more basic construct, the son always wins as the primary authority on everything; the mother smilingly yields to domineering maleness. Every mother welcomes the aggressive infant who "takes hold" and greedily grabs for what he expects and has to have. Strength and determination are signs of health, and mothers make surprisingly little effort to discipline such sons. Couples fight over parental authority, it is true, but the husband's more basic grievance often is that his wife does not relate to him as properly, which is to say as deferentially, as did his admiring mother.

In her article, oddly titled, "The Woman Warrior Versus the Chinaman Pacific," Cheung uses literature for her database, as do many other feminists nowadays. This practice definitely results in a narrowing of feminism to academic or scholarly interests and is not, I think, entirely justified. The woman warrior referred to in Cheung's title is from Maxine Hong Kingston's *The Woman Warrior*, a work which describes "the protagonist's struggle for self-definition amid Cantonese sayings such as 'Girls are maggots in the rice,' 'It is more profitable to raise geese than daughters,' 'Feeding girls is feeding cowbirds.'"

Now, the subject of the difference in attitude of mothers towards daughters and sons is a subject of immense importance to feminist theory. Kingston, says Cheung, is "... accused of falsifying culture and of reinforcing stereotype in the name of feminism." Cheung points out that when Asian American women expose antifemale prejudices in their own ethnic community, the men are likely to feel betrayed, since Asian American men have suffered deeply from racial oppression. Cheung says that "... Kingston reveals not only the similarities between Chinamen's and Chinese women's suffering but also the correlation between these men's umbrage at racism and their misogynist behavior." All of this serves to lead us farther and farther afield from the *feminist* subject at hand, which is the preference of mothers the world over for sons instead of daughters. I would say that what seems to be male tyranny must be viewed not "within the context of racial inequality" but within the context of unequal *authority*.

The son's "tyranny" over the mother is of a much different quality and sort than his tyranny over his wife. *The mother knows that the son is her real property, an asset of her own estate.* The daughter represents *her* own authority and with that authority will come her own estate and wealth in the form of sons of her own. The saying a son's a son until he finds a wife is not true. The son stays with the mother, inherits her estate and brings in a wife who must bow to the mother-in-law. It is the daughter who is thrown out, or sold, or expected to leave, or leaves on her own accord to establish her own domicile. If she is lucky, she finds a spouse whose mother has already died.

There will always be more *regard* for the son than the daughter, even though the mother may deeply empathize with the daughter; after all, she has been there. But we rarely empathize with where we have been and would wish to be no more. Cheung sees the shift from feminist studies to gender studies as indicating that "... the time has come to look at women and men together. ... Expanding the feminist frame of reference will allow certain existing theory to be interrogated or reformulated." I'm afraid "the feminist frame of reference" is far from delineated, nor, I would further claim, can it be manifested anywhere except in the figure and plight of the mother. It is the mother's familiarity with her fate that makes her view her daughter as a hopeless creature, without any intrinsic value to herself or others, except as their unwilling servant.

In my opinion, my son married a Chinese woman for exactly the wrong reason. What he was in love with was the idea of having an obedient and admiring wife. He badly misjudged his Chinese sweetheart; as his wife, to her credit, she has taught him obedience. I admire her for the way she has done this, and I admire my son for falling into domestic line. She married for the wrong reason, too, which was to marry a white professional man. She says her parents virtually instructed her to do this. She is one of three daughters given over to a grandmother who spoke no English, so that both parents could work. With the grandmother's encouragement, my daughter-in-law was able to get a degree that qualified her to teach in elementary schools. (My son is an attorney.) There is no doubt that their two sons will be professional men looking for suitable wives in the not too distant future. I hope they might soon read Kingston's explanation of the term "Chinaman," which their mother has told me many times is comparable to "Nigger."

> The term "Chinaman" has acquired divers connotations through time. In the early days of Chinese American history, men called themselves "Chinamen" just as other newcomers called themselves "Englishmen" or "Frenchmen": the term distinguished them from the "Chinese" who remained citizens of China, and also showed that they were not recognized as Americans. Later, of course, it became an insult. Young Chinese Americans today are reclaiming the word because of its political and historical precision, and are demanding that it be said with dignity and not for name-calling.

Their main problem has been that my son wants to be more than a money-maker: he wants to be the *dominant* parent. Even in the case where fathers or lovers are willing to be less dominant than the mother in guiding and caring for children, the nature of the relationship between the authority (the mother) and the uninformed (the children) is one of challenge if not enmity. Here we see again the futility of words, of being told what is right by the best-intentioned of authorities. As children, we intend and are determined to find out everything for ourselves. The parental example set becomes the deepest influence, as we all know, and yet the example of the mother as glad servant becomes self-defeating in the extreme, in its effect upon daughters and in the habitual expectation it develops in sons. The mother who becomes demanding and puts her own interests ahead of the children is accused of refusing to grow up, of being a not-good-enough mother. A woman cannot undertake parenthood without relinquishing her childhood. However, with the right wife, a man can undertake parenthood without forgoing any of the privileges bestowed upon him as an adored child, or so he expects. I think Cheung has scarcely scratched the surface of the complexity of gender when she ends with the admonishment: "... All of us need to be conscious of our complicity with the gender ideologies of patriarchy, whatever its origins, and to work toward notions of gender and ethnicity that are nonhierarchical, nonbinary, and nonprescriptive; that can embrace tensions rather than perpetuate divisions." I think it more fundamentally important to bore in on the problems of essentialism and the nature of our complicity with the mother and *her authority* whether or not a father is ever found on the scene.

15

Teresa de Lauretis divides her article between a discussion of "Essentialism and Anti-Essentialism" and "Theorizing Beyond Reconciliation." Her claim in the first section at first intrigues, but becomes far too garbled to convince:

> ... barring the case in which woman's "essence" is taken as absolute being or substance in the traditional metaphysical sense (and this may actually be the case for a few, truly fundamentalist thinkers to whom the term essentialist would properly apply), for the great majority of feminists the "essence" of woman is more like the essence of the triangle than the essence of the thing-in-itself: it is the *specific properties* (e.g., a female-sexed body), qualities (as disposition to nurturance, a certain relation to the body, etc.), or necessary attributes (e.g., the experience of femaleness, of living in the world as female) *that women have developed or have been bound to historically, in their differently patriarchal sociocultural contexts, which make them women, and not men.* One may prefer one triangle, one definition of women and/or feminism, to another and, within her particular conditions and possibilities of existence, struggle to define the triangle she wants or wants to be—feminists do want differently. *And in these very struggles, I suggest, consist the historical development and the specific difference of feminist theory*, the essence of the triangle. (My emphasis.)

Ignoring the slur on fundamentalist thinkers, I would counter first that the triangle has no essential function. Woman has. Also, I will leave aside the question whether an abstract idea (triangles do not exist as objects) can be appropriately compared with organic, dynamic systems observable as discrete entities (for example, women and men). It is woman's essential function of motherhood that identifies her as *female.* The function of motherhood (parturition) *proves* that in property, disposition, attribute, and *substance* this entity which functions as a mother is *whole, dynamic, and real.* One could get into discussions of what constitutes a triangle, and how the three line segments comprising a triangle function and so prove themselves to be properly identified as the species "triangle" but it would be quite futile, since triangles do not experience anything, let alone parturition.

With respect to the few "truly fundamentalist thinkers" among whom I would be honored to be numbered, one cannot fairly lump a logically sound *feminist* essentialism based on natural functions far removed from the function of metaphysics, with the New Right bible-thumping reactionaries who worship "holy writ" and the metaphysical faith of our fathers. De Lauretis does point out that few *feminists* "... would deny that feminist theory is all about an essential difference, an irreducible difference, though not a difference between woman and man, nor a difference inherent in 'woman's nature' (in woman as Nature), but a difference in *the feminist conception of woman, women, and the world.*" (My emphasis.) I agree with her when she says that the essential difference of feminism lies, among other things, in its "radical challenge to social life itself." She is also correct in seeing that even as the specific, essential differentiation between feminism and patriarchical masculinism may not be disputed, the question of feminism's specificity, *exactly what comprises the essence of a feminist position*, is the focus of hot debate and wild disagreement. I hope that de Lauretis would readily agree with me that so far as identification goes, feminists must *recognize* that one either is or is not a woman, and that this is as indisputable as whether or not a triangle is or is not a triangle. I believe disputes among feminists hinge on what *the proper function of woman is*. De Lauretis does not face up to this question or any version of it.

Many feminists are now claiming that there is no human function that is "properly" more *hers* than it is *his*. That is getting very near the nub of the matter, but it is also to skip any consideration of the fact that that there is a *categorical difference* between the "proper" function of mothers and the "proper" function of children, who come in two flavors. When one focuses on a radical challenge to social life as currently structured, one is focusing on a new curriculum for *educating the young*. Speaking *as women*, feminists are saying they will no longer be burdened by children. I am saying that mothers and mothers alone will *always* be burdened by children and that the education of children falls entirely to mothers. Categorically, until one becomes a mother, one remains a child.

Although some mothers have lived to regret it, we have turned our children over to the authority of big brothers and to lovers, naming them the father. We have supported and ourselves bowed to the authority and "higher" metaphysical wisdom of the Name of the Father. Feminists are discovering, and documenting, the oppression of this socially embedded authority but they are doing very little by way of analyzing its deepest roots, which is the preference for the son over the daughter in the mother's eyes and heart. Nature proceeds as it always has and always will, but Nature doesn't *care*. Human mothers do. But we don't care for our destiny; we prefer the child who appears to have some other destiny; but all creatures have the *same* destiny which is determined by Nature alone.

Two writings, de Lauretis says, prompted her essay on the uses of essentialism in current feminist critical writing, Chris Weedon's "Feminist Practice and Poststructuralist Theory," and Linda Alcoff's "Cultural Feminism versus Post-Structuralism: The Identity Crisis in Feminist Theory." De Lauretis herself says she will argue that ". . . the essential difference of feminist theory must be looked for in the form as well as the contents of its political, personal, critical, and textual practices." Certainly not in Weedon or Alcoff or in any "poststructuralist theory" that I'm aware of, but more disappointingly, not in de Lauretis' argument, which I couldn't even find, is there any mention of the social intercourse between mother and son as being the grassroots beginning of all social practices. The largest measure of social form and content begin here and it is to this situate we must look if we expect to unravel society's more complex ramifications. Most especially is society's extenuating sexuality rooted in the mother and son dyad.

Textual and contextual human matters begin and end in the home (or the lair, den, or cave) where the authoritative mother produces her constituency. The essentialism of the mother is the essentialism of her parturition, during which act she produces herself in two modes, female and male. The son, not the daughter, fires the *human* mother's imagination. For the *human* mother, the son is more stimulating, more *entertaining* for the very reason that *she sees* he *cannot* become the spitting image of herself. Look! she says to him, you can do anything, go anywhere, discover all there is to discover, see all there is to see. You, my darling son, are my unencumbered self! In the daughter all too readily can be seen the selfsame destiny as the encumbered mother. It is too painful to contemplate. She turns to the son, Do all these wonderful, yet undone things *for me*, see them as I would see them, interpret them with my eyes, think of all the uses that *we* can make of new space, unknown riches, more opportunities, better places to live. Go forth! and I shall longingly await your return; speed, fly away, oh wonderful bird of paradise, be free!

Do today's feminists really want to domesticate sons and lovers? Of course men can care for children, shop, prepare meals, and supervise an estate as well as a woman. It is equally true that women can be adventurer, explorer, inventor, and empire builder, not to mention chief breadwinner and balancer of the checkbook. Indubitably it is also true that women and men dream of doing everything *together.* Aha, that brings us full circle, back to the mother and her constituency. Sons leave home, discover sex, and return to the home of the bride, not to the mother. Daughters leave home and establish their own domicile. Wives give quite different instructions and services to husbands and lovers than mothers give to sons. They expect and get different performances, for the alliance of woman and man as betrothed differs from the alliance of mother and child. The latter represents a much more profound commitment than any made during wedding ceremonies in anticipation of copulation and conjugal love. In ongoing relationships involving two genders, who is serving whom and who is being served by whom and *from what motivation* becomes massively complicated. At the very least, feminists have awakened and are beginning to think seriously about these complications. Feminists, or rather feminist *philosophers*, will need a world of time to unravel and reknit the social fabric of our human world, and I believe philosophers are now in the process of doing that. It could transpire that men will show more desire to be domesticated than women will evince desire to domesticate them.

Patriarchy's incessant use of the trope "man and wife" and the almost incurable coupling of "having a baby" with "getting married and having a baby" are only two examples of social "norms" that are traditional and normative but not descriptively accurate. Let us say that the woman who takes a husband by that act takes unto herself her firstborn, always a male. He becomes the big brother of her family and she delegates all kinds of authority to him. Feminists like de Lauretis are busy imagining and writing about how our human world might work if daughters were a lot more like sons and sons were a little more like mothers. Essentially, it seems to me, what every *adult* human creature must aspire to is to be more like our mother, whose *essential social function* (quite apart from her aforementioned essential biological function of parturition) is to take responsible charge of feeding, clothing, housing, comforting, benignly governing, and thoroughly educating the new generation concerning the facts of life. One fact that is not going to change is that the mother embraces both the son and man and does not consider either a burden. The male is a valuable and tenderly cared-for asset whether he is viewed as a son or a spouse. How the son and the man view the mother is a matter of education. In my opinion, the complexities of sexuality will defeat feminists unless we concentrate on the essentialism of parturition and understand that that is the most important sexual function woman performs. In short, if woman does not function as mother she is not functioning at all, only playing house and dolls (or professor and student, in the case of these academic feminists).

De Lauretis' short second section on feminists being reconciled with one another ends with the recommendation that feminists move on to "a more complex level of analysis," thus overcoming certain impasses. Seen in a larger, *historical* frame of reference, she says, ". . . feminist theory is not merely a theory of gender oppression in culture . . . nor is it the essentialist theory of women's nature." Instead, it is ". . . a developing theory of the female-sexed or female-embodied *social subject* . . . a social subject that is based on its specific, emergent, and conflictual *history*." (My emphasis.) This is a fine point, but the one I found no argument for in de Lauretis' essay. From my view, it seems apparent that the *mother's function* of producing herself in two modes, female and male, has resulted in an unexpected conflict, which is that of the son who would take over the mother's office of authority and the agency of motherhood itself if only he could; but he lacks the *essential substance and body* to do so. *Feminist mothers* I think must sympathize with the desire of sons who see themselves as would-be patriarchs. For similar reasons, I think feminists must be especially sympathetic to homosexual men. Early on, bright children want to do things for themselves. Sons and daughters resent having always to be served and having always to say "thank you" to the mother. We all want to do things *our* way. Perhaps most distressing for men is the onus of "being a man" when their deepest desire is only to be the mother, like the person they love most. She seems to be the one having all the fun attending to the details that make the world a more wonderful place than we could ever have imagined without the example she sets for us. Most abhorrent of all, to civilized sons, must be the idea of aggressively imposing one's will upon another, of inseminating anyone when one's dream is rather to be embraced and inseminated with milky fluid.

The reconciliation I see among feminists and masculinists alike is to be reconciled to the fact that there is such a thing as an authority figure who fills the office of authority and leadership, and that this figure is essentially the mother by virtue of her sexuality and especially her sexual act of parturition. We are bound to the female figure of authority from birth to death. To achieve profundity, feminism as philosophy has only to address female sexuality and to enlighten the world as to how sexuality works in all of its social complexities. There is no symmetry or balance between the two genders, no equality between the mother and her son. Despite the best efforts of sons and patriarchs, the church cannot be mother, the state cannot be mother, no petri dish in a scientific laboratory can be mother. Only the mother who *knows* herself to be mother and all that that implies and entails concerning authority and responsibility can be a truly *human* mother. The Jewish mother may be but a fading image of what the Gentile mother could have been in her ascendancy.

The great cultures of history, most notably the pre-Socratic Greek culture, I view as having feasted off the remains of mother-oriented civilizations. What, I wonder, do academic careerists and feminists think they are renouncing when they renounce any identification with essentialism and its direct connection with motherhood? I read and read, and all I learn from feminist theorists swamped in "scholarship" is that men are the oppressors of women, or that gender itself is the culprit; so let's do away with men and/or with gender, the pouting reasoning goes. Could we please hear from some *real mothers?* That's me, and let me tell you how doomed to failure we are. *Nature* will have its way, and that is something we failures understand rather well. Nothing succeeds like failure, the methodology by which Nature necessarily keeps redoing, restyling, endlessly revising and rerunning the old old story of knowledgeable mothers with their innocent offspring who have everything to learn for themselves.

16

Valerie Smith's article is headed "Split Affinities: The Case of Interracial Rape." She wants to focus on "the centrality within culture of sexual difference" and "to include the putative centrality of racial differences as well." Her position, as I read it, is that the sexual crosslinking of black and white females with black and white males is socially inadmissible *among whites* because of the power struggle of *white* men. She thinks it important for us to recognize "the kinds of silences that structure the social hierarchy in which we live." Facts are ignored in deference to believing the "narrative of myths," she says. The facts are that the majority of rapes committed are intraracial; that rapes by strangers are the least common rapes women experience; and that most rapes are by a man of the woman's race and by a man she knows: her husband, her boss, an acquaintance, or a date. The narrative myths portray the image of sexually inexhaustible black men, the animalism of the black male rapist, and the sexual promiscuity of black females. Smith asserts that such "... Unacknowledged cultural narratives ... which link racial and gender oppression structure our lives; ... the ability of some people to maintain dominance over others depends upon these narratives' remaining pervasive but unarticulated." She cites media treatment of the Central Park assault and rape by a gang of adolescent black youths of a white professional young woman. "The implications of the ways that journalists characterized the young men involved in the Central Park rape become powerfully clear when we juxtapose the reporting of this case with that involving the rape and sexual assault of a 17-year-old 'mildly retarded' white middle-class young woman in northern New Jersey by five, middle-class white teen-age football players ...," she claims.

The bulk of Smith's article recounts how she uses Alice Walker's short story "Advancing Luna" (which involves the rape of a young white female by a young black male in an activist desegregationist peer group) in her classes "... to develop a vocabulary for speaking across differences that are initially the source of silences." Smith's hope was "... that the black students would claim their divergent affinities with the black man on racial grounds and the white woman on the basis of gender, and that the students would recognize the cost of their respective identifications. ... For it was important to me that they acknowledge the implications of their discomfort, the extent to which they felt betrayed by their divisions from each other." She admits that she cannot claim to have achieved either of these goals. "... [T]eaching ... this story has required me to confront the limits of what a class and a syllabus can accomplish," she writes. "Not only were we unable to reach any kind of satisfactory closure in our discussion of "Advancing Luna," but moreover our discussions of subsequent texts did not seem to take place at a heightened level of consciousness." That's quite an admission for an academic feminist to make.

The expectation that we will "locate ourselves in a narrative" is of course a sure bet if the narrative *and the narrator* are fascinating enough. Back I go to harp on what I see as the essential construct of the narrative as well as the model of all education: it is the *believable* mother entertaining her child, or more accurately, indoctrinating her/him with the mother's values; the child sits fascinated, listening, utterly enraptured by the mother's words. When children themselves become the narrators, their *gender* is always of utmost significance, how they see themselves as *either* female *or* male. But the *originary* narrator is always the mother; and how she views her own motherhood will determine what values she passes on to her daughters and sons.

17

Michelle Stanworth's paper, "Birth Pangs: Conceptive Technologies and the Threat to Motherhood," is far from alarmist. It balances the worry that "... the object and the effect of the emergent technologies is to deconstruct motherhood and to destroy the claim to reproduction that is the foundation of women's identity ..." with the new opportunities for infertile women to become mothers. Although fatherhood's control of motherhood is old hat and patriarch scientists may be no different from patriarch theologians, feminists who yell a lot about controlling their own bodies seldom speak of wresting control of motherhood from fatherhood by the simple expedient of identifying themselves with motherhood, except of course in terms of opting to have nothing to do with that institution. Stanworth's article deals with a very different side of this issue: the desire for motherhood of women who are infertile, among which group she places herself. Stanworth says that "... to identify motherhood ... exclusively with nature, with the absence of technology, and indeed, with pregnancy and childbirth runs the risk of blunting the cutting edge of feminist critique." Feminists, she says, "... recognize the pivotal role of motherhood in the subordination of women." Yet, in the face of what is now called "conceptive technologies," Stanworth wonders if "... it is not motherhood per se that we feel the need to preserve." Her final position is that "... The *defense* of motherhood that we ultimately construct will be stronger if we *resist the temptation to use nature as a territory on which to stake our claims.*" (My emphasis.) There is much confusion here.

Stanworth credits "feminist analysis" with rescuing childbearing from the status of the natural, by insisting that pregnancy and childbirth are a sphere of action as "civilized as any of the accomplishments of men." But the attempt "to reclaim motherhood as a female accomplishment need not mean giving the natural priority over the technological—that pregnancy is natural and good, technology unnatural and bad." More confusion. It would seem to me unarguable that mothers and would-be mothers should receive all the help they can get from medical science. Such help would not affect at all the social mores that the authoritative mother establishes for her constituency. Surrogate parents assume the parental office of authority and all of its attendant responsibilities that a natural mother has vacated for whatever reasons. Surely it is a mark of our intelligence as a species that we can bond with children we have not borne.

I have consistently argued that motherhood is not a social "role" but that the essential biological function of parturition endows the mother with inalienable social authority. In view of these biological facts, it makes no sense and is illogical for feminists to "recognize the pivotal role of motherhood in the subordination of women" and it saddens me when a careful writer like Stanworth unthinkingly repeats such a phrase. The natural institution of motherhood is not coterminous with the artificially structured institution of marriage, which definitely is pivotal to woman's social subordination and the undercutting of her authentic authority. Adoptive mothers, no different from natural mothers, can prove their feminist mettle by exerting the *naturally bestowed* authority of mothers over their children and rearing them according to feminist values, the first tenet of which is the primacy of the female. Male surrogates become females so far as performing familial social services go. Until all women take motherhood seriously, men will not take all women seriously. Conceptive technologies reflect the male scientist's fascination with life. Perhaps women are less fascinated than men with the rudiments of biological conception and gestation because they have no intimate experience of the process. In view of certain strains of anti-essentialism among feminists, I would offhand consider feminism more a threat to motherhood than conceptive technologies, but let us continue to assume in good faith that everyone is still pretty much for motherhood, the flag, and apple pie.

18

Carla Freccero's "Notes of a Post-Sex Wars Theorizer" ranges over what may be described as preferred ways of experiencing sexual orgasm as *lifestyles* protected, or *theoretically protectable* under state laws as either long honored tradition or a defendable civil right. She lets a hooker speak for herself, employs Margaret Atwood's *The Handmaid's Tale* to depict the reality of female slavery and the sometime consequences of "state protection," and probes deeply into the complexities of pornography and sado/masochistic sexual desires. Freccero sees the feminist movement and feminist thinking as having

"...the potential to conceive action and analysis in staggerlngly revolutionary terms." There are tactical priorities, she says, and none of them is strictly sexual: imperialism, class stratification, and the conditions of the neediest women in the United States. She approvingly quotes Betty Friedan's 1985 reaction to feminism's deep divide over the issue of pornography: "Get off the pornography kick and face the real obscenity of poverty." In my opinion, Freccero's article is the most troubling but also probably the most on-target contribution to *Conflicts in Feminism.* The conflicts Freccero lists and details in a most helpful way amount to *war among feminists.* This war which began in the eighties is still raging in the nineties. It's too bad that the war is all about *sexual* proclivities, seen as the hot desire of females to *enjoy* sex one way or another. No one, of course, is going to take such sound advice as Friedan offers the least bit seriously. Nor, I daresay, will any sex-driven feminist or intellectually-minded theorist pause to consider the highly evolved *natural connection* between sexuality and motherhood.

If feminism is a theory of sexuality and feminism's chief complaint is that woman's sexuality has been maliciously *suppressed, exploited, and misinterpreted*, it would follow that feminism itself should be able to inform us concerning the facts of female sexuality and woman's true desires. Freccero informs us of the fierce infights among feminists regarding female sexual desire and pleasure as they are lived today. With the spread of brass and leather S/M exploits among lesbian lovers, no longer can the oppositional view of male and female hold, whereby "an aggressive, predatory, dehumanizing masculinity is opposed to a nurturant, humanizing, egalitarian, peaceful femininity," if indeed it ever did hold. Female sexuality has always been seen as a threat to man, as witness Rousseau's *Emile.* Cora Kaplan, reports Freccero, traces the genealogy of the disputes in contemporary feminist sexual ideologies to the liberal Rousseau's conclusive analysis, where "the possibility of women's civil, economic and psychological independence is rejected because it would also enable the independent and licentious exercise of her supposedly insatiable appetite." Freccero gives additional historic views on woman's sexuality, from Mary Wollstonecraft to Bill Moyers and the infamous 1965 Moynihan Report. Freccero highlights the fact that "good girl/bad girl" splits always find a place within political traditions. It seems evident that political traditions however decadent or exploitive reserve a pool of sexually pure "good" girls for the important business of civilized motherhood. Here, pleasure for its own sake and orgasm for its own reward becomes sexual duty for its own sake and orgasm for the reward of a child, leaving the virgin bride quite as debased and controlled by man as the whore. Freccero ends her paper with a strong emphasis on Third World women where the "politics of sexuality" among feminists centers around sexual violence itself and not about women's sexual desires or pleasures.

If it wasn't obvious before, Freccero's article makes it obvious that feminism does not have a theory of sexuality. I submit, that when feminism is able to work on establishing one, it will be a theory of motherhood. The glories of passionate orgasm are exactly what the human mother knows a lot more about than do her maturing offspring. The human mother all too easily and accurately projects what will happen when a certain inevitable stage of biological development ensues among her underlings. Freud did not do as much as he might have in pointing to the mother as the basic *problematic* sex object for the *son.* The Greek tragedians seem totally to have messed up the real message of Oedipus Rex: man is married to his mother whether or not the *idea* of this *fact* drives him crazy. It is the *mother* that man the son is so intent on keeping sexually pure. Up to the present moment, the best of epistemologists—for example Helen Longino, Joseph Rouse, and Philip Kitcher—persist in structuring human knowledge as though we come from cabbages (or some other source as obscure as god almighty). No intellectual female or male, feminist or chauvinist, seems able or willing to face the raw fact that we originate from our mothers. Evidently that is simply too embarrassing or unthinkable. Now that we are grown up and sexually sophisticated, the reasoning seems to go, it is downright impossible that our mother still knows more than we know. Horrors, wouldn't that indicate that she herself consorted sexually with untold others? Unthinkable! Revolting! Disgusting!

A conspiracy of denial exists between mothers and children concerning the mother's overt sexuality. Nowhere is this denial more pronounced than among philosophers and intellectuals, including academic feminists. Scientists stay far afield of the sticky subject, studiously concentrating on emotionally safer behavioral patterns of things like gene expression or particle physics. All sexual desire is nature's ploy and prelude to reproductive entrapment. No female with the tiniest piece of foreknowledge would volunteer to leave childhood for motherhood. We move along nature's biological conveyor belt and give our passage all kinds of entertaining narrative, comforting stories, and imaginary meanings. There is no meaning to any reality; we along with all other creatures and things are only the means by which there is something instead of nothing at all. In this knowledge, human mothers have learned to accept their inevitable motherhood. That is why we comfort, entertain, and attempt to civilize the young. At first view, it seems better than jungle life. But perhaps mothers are wrong for with puberty animal sexual glands take over her beautifully civilized kids and all hell breaks loose. The human love they have known together is a celibate love; the reality they seek now is rife with delicious, wicked sex. Who needs a celibate mother? What a dreary model, what a naive old fogey. Far more important to understand than *sex* a la Freud or *child development* a la Spock is the complex process of *mother* development. When and how we learn about the sexuality of our mother is secondary to when and how *she* learns about her *own* sexuality. Some mothers never learn so controlled are they by religious and social mores. But in the quietude of their own reminiscences, most mothers I think *know.* All of this knowledge is of no avail of course to randy feminists who are out for their own justification and pleasure. Pleasure justifies a lot. The pleasure of being sovereign over one's own children justifies a lot. But no theory of sexuality is going to stop the conveyor belt Nature has us on. Change is in the doing but alackaday we never realize what we are doing, only what we have done. It's the same old story: hindsight is great.

19

Marnia Lazreg is an Algerian sociologist interested in feminist theory and epistemology. Teaching at Hunter College and writing about women and the contradictions of Islamic socialism, she most recently has published "Gender and Politics in Algeria: Unravelling the Religious Paradigm." Her article in *Conflicts in Feminism* is entitled "Feminism and Difference: The Perils of Writing as a Woman on Women in Algeria." Lazreg's gripe is with feminists in France and the U. S. who, she claims, assume a condescending attitude towards all other women. She begs for a bond based not on difference but likeness. She comes close to suggesting that all women are the same but she does not venture to say exactly how.

Lazreg misses many golden opportunities to name the essentialism of motherhood as binding together the identity and experience of women and I find it disappointing that she fails to do so. Lazreg's mixed bag of literature (opening with Omar Khayyam and closing with Shakespeare), sociology (Max Weber, Emile Durkheim, C. Wright Mills) anthropology (Bronislaw Malinowski), philosophy (Husserl, Heidegger), and religion (Rosemary Reuther, Margaret Smith), to name but a few among many, amply demonstrates that "Making a distinction as to who is and is not a feminist . . . has become nearly futile." She seems to think it important to know, but who really cares? U. S. academic feminism's market for "Middle Eastern women" is such, she claims, that even writers who do not profess to feminism feel free to borrow its language: "private sphere," "sexual segregation," and "women's subordination," for example.

The point, she says, is neither to subsume other women under one's own experience nor to uphold a separate truth for "them." It is to allow "them" to *be* while recognizing that what "they" are is as valid and comprehensible as what "we" are. "'They' are not the antithesis of ourselves *that justifies our studying 'them' in ways we do not study ourselves.*" (My emphasis.) This is surely true and a perfect setup to deliver the punch line on the universality of motherhood, but Lazreg makes no move to do so. I think that very odd.

Lazreg wants feminism to reorient its thinking towards humanism and she recommends Heidegger's letter on humanism as posing the kinds of questions that might be probed, viz, What is woman's/man's place in history? *"A new humanism requires a more original reexperiencing of what it is to be human,"* contends Lazreg. (My emphasis.) I would counter that a *new* humanism will be raised under the flag of a *genuine feminism.* Though Lazreg clearly sees that the feminist "... propensity to apprehend social reality in terms of binary oppositions is a contradictory element in feminist thought," she falls back on what she calls "the crucial issue of *intersubjectivity.*" (Her emphasis.) She reasons that "For the intersubjective component of experience to become evident in *the study of difference within and between genders*, a certain form of humanism must be reaffirmed. But the rejection of humanistic philosophy, which subsumed woman under man while making claims to universalism, has so far been replaced with *the essentialism of difference.*" (My emphasis.) "But," she wants to know, and I along with her, "what does antihumanism offer 'different' peoples? On what grounds ... can powerless people struggle against their relegation to the prison house of race, color, and nationality into which antihumanism locks them?"

I wish I could impress upon Lazreg and others that the essentialism of the mother is *not an essentialism of difference.* On the contrary, it is the mother's true seeing of herself as constituting a *unity* with her children, female and male, that gives *our species* its *human* characteristic of *unified intelligence whose essence reflects the mother's integrating function.*

In short, without the *essential integrity of our human mother's intelligence,* there can be no characteristically *human* species. A repression of one's motherhood, if one is born woman, is a repression of one's human intelligence.

In her notes, Lazreg states that she is working on a "methodology rooted in Husserlian phenomenology." This I believe could prove spectacularly successful if she would just think to *adopt the mother as the noumenal bracketing of human reality* as well as *the context within which evidence of "difference" emerges.* I greatly lamented what I instead read: "The collapse of the colonial empires, the rise of consumer societies, and the crises of the late capitalist states have formed the context within which assertions of 'difference' have emerged. The celebration of difference between women and men, homosexuals and heterosexuals, the mad and the sane, has since become the unquestioned norm." This may be factual in an historical or sociological sense, but there is an unquestioned norm that transcends all history and social variables and that is the normal mother and her essential function of regenerating life. Lazreg's search for "a common denominator between people of different cultures, a *human* bond," can find a happy ending in essentialism properly understood and, to boot, feminism will at last have a bona fide theory.

Despite Lazreg's chiding, she moves us no nearer to a feminist phenomenology or theory than any of the others. The feminist fear of essentialism centers around the fear that a unique female "nature" will further alienate woman from man's more admirable "nature" as characterized by his mind and intellectual prowess. Essentialism as a theory simply states that in the female's unique sexuality, that is, in its overarching function of motherhood, both female and male genders are unified and have their being. Furthermore, every human relationship takes the form of the mother-and-child relationship. In the biological world of living species there are no other connective constructs possible. I'm all for a feminist phenomenology that makes the mother's experience of noumenology, of knowing and experiencing the thing-in-itself, comprehensible and embraceable. If Lazreg is game to undertake such an assignment, I can point to some pitfalls, things to look out for. One pitfall is that although it is vehemently denied by *everybody*, throughout their lives *sons as a category* continually have to maintain their access which is to say their *connection* to the mother. In doing this, they blind themselves in good Oedipal fashion to the fact that all women are mothers. Sons have little difficulty finding sisters to conspire with them in this myth. Another pitfall is that although human love appears celibate, the mother/child connection epitomizes sexuality in its most dynamic manifestation. As someone observed, I think it was J. D. Salinger, as he observed a nursing child, there was god pouring herself into god, keeping heaven and hell going, so to speak.

Men are much too seared by female betrayal to entirely trust woman's embrace, most especially when we exhibit a passionate desire to open up and give all, no strings attached. Man, not unintelligently, has learned to make sure that he does the embracing. He will no longer be the petitioner but the grantor of favors, nay, of the very necessities of life. The screw has turned and mother/woman gasps and screams, indeed we are dying under the niggardly largesse of hurt but shrewdly self-protective sons. Meanwhile, mother/woman, split and divided by the son's craven fear of incest, has learned from him that schizophrenia is the most expedient way to get even a crumb of his stingy largesse: as whore denying her motherhood and/or as virgin denying her sexuality. It is understandable even in Freudian terms that we all feel betrayed by the "thrownness" from the given mother during parturition; the traumas of birth and weaning cannot be wholly healed, for it is also a thrownness to death as Heidegger didn't exactly see in this context, but should have, in my opinion. The taboo of incest creates *for the manchild* a third trauma. Just as he begins to regain trust in the mother's tender love, if indeed she hasn't committed the final betrayal somewhere along the line by sickening and dying when he was in direst need, he discovers that she is quite useless to him sexually. Again he is propelled away from the one he loves most. The result is that man has been forced to essentialize *difference*: first the difference between "wife" and "mother"; but wife soon enough *becomes* mother in the happily married son's life. So again he essentializes *difference,* this time the profound difference between "wife" and "whore" (or mistress), the faithful wife having assumed a persona as sacred as and indeed identical with the mother's. Notwithstanding all of these niceties, among women there is no *essential* difference, nor is there any *essential* difference among sons and lovers. The difference in *function* between the mother/wife/whore/mistress/sister and the son/husband/lover/father /brother is not an *essential* difference. One gets into social "roles" here, and roles involve social storytelling. The two genders remain *one kind of being* (we hope, *human*).

Lazreg has more to say about discourse and storytelling than I have here indicated. Like other academics, she regularly invokes both Foucault and Derrida. Her final question is a quote from Dostoevsky's *Notes from the Underground*: ". . . Isn't the whole point to have a *voice?*" No, I think rather not. From where I'm observing, the essential point for man seems to be to have and to cling to a mother, and for the mother the essential point seems to be to bear and release children to ever new horizons. Another essential point is that wheresoever children find themselves, mothers will be there also, for releasing is not the same thing as forsaking. As in every case that is dynamically sound and *true*, Nature's way of doing things warrants this universal sequence of events; generally we can rely upon mothers and surrogate parents dying, leaving the young alone and on their own, and not always or necessarily bereft.

20

The subject of essentialism comes up in *Conflicts in Feminism*'s last article, "Criticizing Feminist Criticism," an edited transcript of three feminists conversing over each other's feminist views and positions (the three are Jane Gallop, Marianne Hirsch, and Nancy K. Miller). Other subjects covered are authority, power, race, separatism, and something called feminist "positioning," along with the inevitable Lacan and deconstruction and their supposed influence on feminism. A good deal of the exchange is about feminists fairly criticizing or "trashing" other feminists, depending on whose ox was gored. It seemed strange that, according to the editors, "... The fact that Gallop ... criticized Hirsch and Miller and ... managed nevertheless to continue her friendship with them ... gave this conversation its promise." But, it turns out, according to Hirsch, "... there is now a way of building a career on trashing feminist work. I feel like a lot of conversations are getting cut off by using ... "club" words—essentialism or things like that.... You say these words, people get defensive, and nothing happens further."

"It's all about being right and wrong," says Jane.

"What's the right feminist position?" asks Nancy. "Who decides what's wrong or right and is that decision being made within feminism or outside of feminism?"

Nancy confesses that she used to think that separatism was a bad idea, "But now I think the most radical thought feminism ever had was separatism." Jane counters that feminism should not go back to separatism because "one can never simply go back to a position." Nancy opines that "Separatism has been translated into 'essentialism'." "In fact, it has become a positive embarrassment to talk about women." She reports that when she ended a speech with, "I hope we are becoming women," she was attacked by one of the strongest voices of anti-essentialism, Denise Riley, who reportedly said the worst thing we could be was women. Marianne queries, "So what's at stake? ... we've also all been taught that polemic is great." Jane: "I hate being attacked by other feminists ... I also find ... conflict with other women difficult. Conflict with men, I actually find somewhat pleasurable." Nancy: "I've seen Stanley Fish ... go through an amazingly brutal exchange of assaults and then walk off, and it's as if he'd played a squash game and then went home to take a shower. That is something that most women don't know how to do. I certainly don't." Jane: "... what happens when you turn ... from men to women? ... What happens if I turn from people who are clearly more powerful than I to people who are the same or less powerful?" Nancy: "My way of looking at this is to see it as a question of positioning: are you the same as or different from? and how do you show this?" "One of the things that makes feminism particular is a self-consciousness about ways of knowing and the ways in which we believe what we know. Is it possible ... to think about some kind of pedagogy or some kind of way of being that would break the cycle of trashing the predecessor, killing the mother?" Jane: "I think it hasn't happened because, first of all, the reticence to recognize the power of the mothers has made it hard to talk about.... The only alternatives proposed are filial piety or killing the mother. The filial piety model actually reinforces the Oedipal structure.... The daughter graduate student trying to gain a voice for herself must kill the mother if that is the expectation. I think we need to make it all explicit and deal with it and then say, 'wait a minute; this is a totally impossible alternative.'"

The exchange is replete with whatever fork one wants to take in pursuit of consuming feminist enlightenment.

Feminists it seems would prefer to join science and religion in refusing to admit or consider that enlightenment has a politics. Philosophy is a little more borderline, some straightforwardly political and some purportedly more open and searching. No one in any of these voluble camps would seriously argue that Nature is capable of a political ploy or position of any kind but none of the camps wants to be tied in solely with Nature. Indeed, Nature does not enlighten us so much as we enlighten ourselves, albeit as a *natural process*, in terms of what happens to us in our natural habitat, our body. We handily forget that political maneuvering is tied to our *awareness* of Nature, that is, to basic facts regarding our survival which we cannot forget. It becomes our "second nature" to be political, once we become cognizant of our existential predicament. What I would ask feminists to analyze first is the essential difference between the mother's existential predicament and the child's. The essential difference between female and male problems of survival must be analyzed after the first analysis is complete.

True knowledge that makes us purportedly free of error—versus the bondage of ignorance, superstition, and false belief—seems the rallying cry of everyone who can think and *speak*. If it weren't for language, I wouldn't be troubled with hearing about your insights and why you are so convinced that what you see or conclude is valid; nor would you be pained by hearing my accounts of reality and truth. We could proceed through life like the speechless animals we used to be, taking care of ourselves as best we can and letting Nature take its course without thought or ceremony, politics, or philosophical disputes. Via language, *men* circumvent difficulties in understanding or accepting Nature "as is," especially in connection with the mother, by establishing a creation "story" congenial to social applications of whatever conduct they wish to impose. The Judaic/Christian story of creation remains in place as applied to the human family, wherein man is the master and rightful head of "his" woman and her children. This construction of the family is achieved through *speech*. What feminism glaringly lacks is a creation story. Interestingly enough, the conflicts raging among feminists are over *how* woman is made, *where* she comes from in people's *minds*, including women's own minds.

No one wants to believe in a unique female nature, and I do not want to, either. But I am forced to believe in a unique *function* which is fairly labeled "female." When any object demonstrates a capacity to undergo parturition, leaving after its own death a recognizable version of itself which proceeds to repeat the life cycle of the departed one, that object represents a *dynamic* system labeled and known as "female" *identified by* its characteristic function. Thus, it's easy to see how a unique function gets translated as a unique nature. Despite labeling, the female biological process, in which the male function is *included*, is independent of speech and goes on regardless of how it is nominally understood and explained. No speech act or creation story can modify or refigure the process simply by claiming that the female function is included as a small afterthought, a rather insignificant and some say inordinately troublesome part of *male essentialism*. While males do not possess a female function, they cannot be said to have a nature in any way different from the female who bore them, so it is reasonable to give up the uniqueness of a female or male nature in favor of what is seen as human equality. A great deal of feminist writing has been spent trying to achieve this very understanding, but with little success. The unique function of the mother gets thrown out with the "inequality" bathwater, but feminism is left with really nothing to discuss other than egalitarian careers and egalitarian politics. *Adult* women and men living together, learning together, and reproducing together might go far together were it not for *the offspring of females* who prove very disruptive to this egalitarian paradise. *Males do not bear offspring.* Males can be corralled and trained to take part in civilized community life as structured by the long-suffering mothers, but their hearts aren't in it. The heart of the average male glows with the passion of competition, of being simply the *strongest*, and of governing or rather, dominating by muscle alone. This is the alpha male syndrome that works among nonhuman animals but has proved unworkable in our species, as a result I think of the intelligence of the human mother, who prefers intelligent sons and lovers over stupid ones who rely upon brute strength to keep dumb females "in line."

Nevertheless, if feminism as a philosophy can teach us anything I would think it would be the message that as creatures *we are bound to Nature*. We are not free to change the rules by which Nature controls its own being. Creatures can build nests, lairs, hives, homes, and in many ways enhance a closure, making its interior environment more comfortable and safe from enemies who would devour us, and less vulnerable to Nature's assaults and merciless forces. Creatures cannot change the fact that females bear offspring and males do not. Feminist philosophy must clarify the situation of mothers. Motherhood is servitude but the mother only appears to be the child's servant. As I've explained elsewhere, the intelligent mother understands that she is serving herself. Yet, the human mother is the originary creature who decides to intervene with Nature and to demand a surcease to *abject* servitude. Men are most often faulted for such originary intent to intervene with Nature for selfish reasons, but as usual woman got there first. The human mother tries to teach her offspring some manners. As time transpired, her male offspring tried to change the whole scenario, eventually claiming (such is the miracle of words) that he has no *essential* use for the mother; god together with technology will supply all of his truly *essential* needs which are definitely not material but instead *entirely spiritual.* The results are, that while it may be *logically and scientifically sound* for man to claim that it is "nature's way" for woman to be wasted by her young and die in servitude to future mankind, it is *not* logically or scientifically sound and in fact quite cheating and dishonorable *for man to claim that he has no* essential *need for the mother, that his god alone suffices, thank you very much.*

Feminism I'm sorry to say is far from segueing into an harmonious whole the complex orchestrations of civilization's unity of purpose, at least from the viewpoint of mothers: to make our *natural* creaturely world safer, more comfortable, and *entertaining.* One is hard put to find any statement that might accurately describe man's idea of civilization. One can only suspect that it is patterned after the above-mentioned alpha male syndrome with god somehow used as a fence to support "Nature's way" as interpreted by males who resist the civilizing efforts of mothers, preferring their own bullying techniques. Bullying techniques work, the locker-room argument goes, women love it, and who can quarrel with success? Any feminist theory must derive, I submit, from the *mother's experience* of motherhood. My experience *with* my mother and my experience *as* a mother are exactly where segueing, philosophically, must be harmonized and *theoretically understood* as a necessary harmonizing. It is *as a mother* that woman first encounters her son, and the two become lovers. It is that mother/son love that keeps female and male bound naturally together *as civilized human beings*. Any true commonality of experience among *men as human beings* necessarily reverts and reduces to one's experience with the mother. Among women, commonality of experience with the mother is normally superseded by commonality of experience *as* a mother. It is too often forgotten that men as "fathers" have no common *experience* as have women as *mothers*. The bonding of men *against* women is the bonding of males who love to fight it out among themselves in expectation that the females will be in the wings, panting to copulate with the biggest bully, and there is clearly no shortage of females standing there, panting. In contradistinction to *mothers,* women who have not yet experienced parturition likewise have no mutual *experience* upon which essential *existential* data might be compared.

Parturition is more than a profound experience; it radically changes the female's position in relation to herself; she is no longer child but suddenly an adult authority. However she structures the world, whatever story she tells, it will be accepted and believed by the child. Across the board, feminists are embroiled in the question, Does *how I am seen* really affect how I see myself? Of course it does, but this "external" control by an "other" originates in the mother/child relationship at a point where the child could not possibly be *seeing* the mother at all. It is *her gaze* upon her child and *her realization* of her/his *expectations* that *she cannot be* less *than friend* that change the whole scene. Indeed, I consider it indisputable that it is *that gaze containing that realization* that makes us human. (I consider Lacan so far off-base as not to be worthy of discussion; the originary gaze is totally genderless and *for that reason* is totally human.) It seems to me that feminists understand neither *function* in a naturalistic sense, nor *ideas* in a philosophical sense. The distinction between the two is crucial and not one that has always been crucially marked among philosophers, or scientists for that matter. Ideas divide, whereas functions unify. It should come as no surprise that feminists filled with pride over their "ideas" find themselves divisive and at each other's throats.

Who remains *friends?* Not often mother and child. Not usually the ambitious student and the master. Even today one cannot be both a Platonist and an Aristotelian, a Jew and a Christian. I either like or don't like what I *hear.* I also either like or don't like what I see, smell, and touch. Color is not an idea, but it divides visual tastes. Taste as in the mouth is not an idea, but one of the two most empirical realities there is, the other being touch. As I see things, the rock-bottom issue is the certain knowledge that one has concerning one's own motherhood. Whereof one knows nothing, thereof one should not speak, and that goes for academic women and feminists speaking for mothers. If they *are* mothers and so functioning, let them so speak. No one needs to hear anything more from the fathers, or anything said in the Name of the Father. To our very own sons, no doubt we will listen and heed, or at least take note. Mothers are incapable of bonding *against men* in any manner similar to the way men bond against women. In other words, mothers do not bond against sons nor men against their mothers. There is a world of difference between not being friends and being *enemies.* When sons become strange "men" to women other than their mother, and mothers become even stranger "women" to men other than their sons, human reality splits and falls apart. What can glue it back together? A genuine feminist philosophy, I hope. Feminism has not yet achieved a mainstream philosophical position but when it does it likely will be adjudicated as a political position and not as a body of axiomatic knowledge based upon natural processes and having little to do with speech or discursive pastimes. This judgment will be overcome in time as feminist theory proves itself in practice, but then again the practice will be a *political* praxis insofar as social institutions, services, ceremonies, entertainments, and celebrations become oriented to the civilizing values of mothers, and the murderous competitions of warring brothers will be long forgotten.

Summary

My criticism of *Conflicts in Feminism* hopes to convince the authors and readers that a sound feminist philosophy can derive only from the biology of motherhood and not "from the place of feminism" (or of masculinism). In their Conclusion, editors Keller and Hirsch point out that many of the authors envisioned "the place of feminism" in spatial terms. All speak in support of "the interests of women" and each strives for "an approach that would encourage dialogue and conversation among opposing factions." Precisely the theme running through my criticism is that it is woman's and man's logical connection to *motherhood* that stays firmly in place. This sensible and unopposable connection to the mother must be correctly understood before feminism as a *unifying philosophy* can take root and flourish. The fact that we *psychologically* oppose the mother and her authority is of immense philosophical importance, for such subjects as incest, which is taboo, and man's freedom and autonomy, which are popular and endlessly flaunted, are implicated in our psychological negativism towards the mother.

Motherhood is not an ideology, as is fatherhood. Motherhood is the harshest of facts. *Modern mothers* must probe more deeply into their motherhood in order to reach a deeper comprehension of our special allegiance to sons and by extension, men. This may seem a far cry from current philosophies of mathematical knowledge (for instance, Philip Kitcher's) and epistemologies based upon scientific knowledge (for instance, Helen Longino's). However, I see a close connection between the extensive support males habitually expect and invariably receive from females for *any* endeavor males choose to undertake, from purest mathematics to the most obscene pornography, and the human mother's remarkable perception of herself in the two modes she produces of herself, female and male. The only space we can know about, it seems to me, is constrained by our *human* perception of it. Perception itself is a function of organismic survival. Lifestyle and perception being inextricably commingled, it behooves philosophy to examine very carefully the differences in sexual lifestyles of women and men as a prelude to undertaking an examination of possibly basic differences in perceived reality between the two genders. To know thyself surely is to understand one's sexuality and how it works in relation to the larger system which encompasses both genders. The largest question philosophy can ask (and Immanuel Kant asked it) is *how* an organism's cognition of its dynamic processes might exceed the bounds of its own sensory experience.

My hope is to push feminists, especially feminists who are mothers, toward philosophy and its age-old problems, the chief of which is man's acquisition of knowledge. Any solution to a problem whose problemization itself is questionable seems wildly unlikely. The idea that man is woman's oppressor has little to recommend it as a philosophical problem. I would direct feminists to a more restricted place, where even the great Kant found himself constrained. One of Kant's deeper insights was that the knowing subject understands only what the mind produces after a plan of its own, so the problem of knowledge can be resolved only if the subject produces its object. Prior to Kant, the Italian philosopher, Vico, had said it even more succinctly: man understands only what he makes. My platform for feminism rests on the biological facts that by producing men and *idealizing* them as free and therefore unlike herself, mothers do men *and mothers* a disservice. It is indisputable that mothers perceive man's sexual connection to woman more fully than do children or men. Self-knowledge being the basis of all human knowledge, it behooves women who are not yet mothers to address their questions to mothers, and not to join with men in trying to solve (or more likely, deny) problems according to a plan of their own making that excludes or selectively ignores the overarching sexuality of womanhood.

All questions regarding the external world are originally addressed to the mother, and rightly so. Civilization depends upon her ability to integrate all knowledge to the task at hand, which is to live as long as possible in health and familial happiness. A good deal like children, men take familial happiness for granted, overlooking the facticity of the overburdened mother's perception of familial reality. I fail to see how feminist *scholarship* can contribute to philosophical thought short of scrutinizing and subsequently speaking more or less from the mother's point of view. I do not disdain feminist scholarship, far from it. Much of it is brilliant, a fine example being Kathleen Jones' research on gender, authority, and sovereignty, first published in the Spring 1991 issue of the journal *Differences* under the title "The Trouble with Authority." Like Helen Longino, Janet Kourany, Pamela Hall, and a host of others, she wants nothing to do with what is seen as essentialism. Jones missed a great opportunity, after giving a stunning Hobbesian account of monarchal authority as unified and *sovereign,*to point out that human mothers function as sovereign monarchs. Instead, Jones ends her article by proclaiming that *no one* acts the part of the sovereign. According to the article, everyone simply engages in political action, following rules and inventing others as we go along, unafraid of uncertainty, and so imaginative and creative are we as individuals that we are never stuck in any particular world. (I respond to Jones' comprehensive and fascinating article in another paper.)

My purpose in writing a mother-oriented philosophy is to make the case for mothers, who are uniquely *unburdened* by problems of identity or gross misunderstanding concerning their all-encompassing female sexuality: mothers know *who* they are and they understand *what* they are for. Now it may be that mathematicians and scientists know who mathematicians and scientists are and even what they are for, but before we can be certain of those identities and functions as being *nontrivial* identities and functions, philosophy must offer us a clearer identity and understanding of the mother (woman) in contradistinction to her son, the manchild. My contention is that as a result of wrongheaded notions of who the father is and what he is for, philosophy, science, and math have misdirected their inquiries concerning what we can know and how we can know it. That is, male interests seem quite barren of any important social significance other than political, academic, or religious status and power, definitely unhelpful when it comes down to the most important business of all, which is familial health and happiness. To survive, it is imperative that women and men understand exactly what we must do and why, in order to live in familial health and happiness, together and severally. If philosophy, math, and science cannot contribute to these social goals, then they are of marginal value to civilization, it would seem to me.

The idea of fatherhood deceptively simplifies the immense logical complexities of motherhood, which is not an idea but a fact. The facts which the contributors of *Conflicts of Feminism* most often cite and rely upon for identification and mutuality of interest are not drawn from the physical facticity of motherhood. The authors resort to social abstractions such as "oppression" and "struggle," which can be given true enough economic particularity with suggestions for remedy, but it is not likely that the burden of motherhood which Nature puts upon woman alone can or should be remedied. Therefore, I have pressed for a thoroughgoing analysis of motherhood and have hinted that women who have not gone through parturition may be as incapable as their brothers of understanding what it is like to be in *that place*. It seems apparent that the quite limited self-understanding of many feminists derives its perspective from the child's place, making feminism little different from masculinist humanism. Kathleen Jones speaks of "contentious struggles for authority" among feminist writers and researchers. My point is that the mother's *place* is coextensive with the *office* of authority. It is this *office* that fatherhood would take as its own. Man would not dream of relinquishing his vaunted male freedom for motherhood and all the self-sacrificing drudgery that it entails. Man does not want his mother to be a drudge; his solution has been to enslave others to serve her (and especially her surrogate, the wife). Thus classism and racism are born, for one cannot enslave members of one's own "race" but one can with impunity enslave an "inferior race."

The transfiguration of female modality from the mother in the child to the mother with child, who potentially is also mother with child, and so on, is a dynamic process. Historically, men have had difficulty seeing their proper place in these proceedings and now women as well are indicating difficulty in seeing themselves as representing the *maternal* dynamic upon which human life depends. One cannot blame female children for wanting to continue in the privileged position that childhood gives them, but that's not the way motherhood works. Unlike motherhood, fatherhood is little more than an extension throughout man's adult life of the male child's privileged position of freedom, which in essence is freedom from motherhood. A man simply takes a wife who continues to mother him in ways not at all different from the mother's devoted attentions. Although the son can replace his mother by finding another female who will baby him, eventually he will resent being always the obedient baby and never the sovereign mother.

Investigation of this psychological resentment of the mother, and indeed of any authority figure, prevalent among men (and now women too) seems to me crucial to future philosophical investigations concerning perceived reality as well as desirable social goals. It is not surprising that many men resort to aggressive tyranny and inauthentic dominance of some kind, nor is it so surprising that many women welcome the dominance of men. The woman who bears one or more children may reject motherhood and its office of authority, doing everything her intellect and charm allow to insure that she may remain a child. Romantically attaching oneself to a supportive man who promises to baby you seems a sure bet to lots of young females. Such innocents are nonetheless doomed to assuming (with the help of servants, one prays) the domestic responsibilities of authority figures in full charge of their self-produced constituencies so far as the necessities of human life go (food, clean clothes and habitat, love, and the *identity* of *belonging*).

Intelligent human mothers gain enormous insight into the profound differences between being a child and being a *functioning* mother. Motherhood forces upon woman a fundamental shift of functional relationships; she moves from the predicate position of the known child, to the position of the knowing subject who recognizes her own child as object and property of herself. Until she experiences her own parturition, daughters are not likely to understand themselves as the property of their mother, any more than sons are likely to see themselves as the property of their mother (or wife, same thing). During the time new mothers are desperately learning what it is to be strong as an adult, they have to pretend that they know what they're doing and can do it. It makes children exceedingly anxious and nervous to see mothers uncertain and confused, and the same goes for professors and students. However, when mothers for whatever reasons no longer are expected to function as the human community's wisest, most authoritative, most caring, trustworthy adults, decadence and disintegration have their heyday. The most dedicated, professed "professional" professors cannot fill the gap left by mothers abdicating their sovereign responsibilities. The pit of hell is where mothers, clinging to their own childhood, despise and neglect their motherhood.

No amount of professorial goodwill among philosophers and scientists, and the religious for that matter, however much they claim to *care* about societal problems and needs, can serve to displace the authority of mothers who unquestionably are often just plain wrong, but so are philosophers and scientists who posture pretentiously and not always, in my view, persuasively concerning the degree to which they "care."

Feminism's work is cut out for itself: to explain the basic authority of mothers in terms of *biological* facts. When one becomes a mother, assertion of one's own authority becomes mandatory, with the young mother herself issuing the mandate to constituent members. Most family members gladly recognize that Mom's boss, but husbands often resist her authority *especially in public.* However that may be, the point is that *human* motherhood gives *human* life its *cognitive* point and purpose. Everyone at some point wonders why we can't conduct ourselves amorally, like animals live, untroubled by human virtues. "I am tired of the gender of things," Anne Sexton wrote, making much the same point, I think. The depressing necessity of being one gender or the other is, I submit, the depressing human knowledge that one must be either mother or child. Child may seem preferable when one is distraught mother, but mother seems better when one is doomed to eternal childhood. Still, I see the place of objective knowledge (knowledge of objects in the external world) and mathematical constructs of these entities as extremely crucial to the life and understanding of individuals, female and male, as well as of mothers, whose responsibility it is to care for us and to inform us concerning the ways of the big, bad world. If one of the functions of philosophy is advisory, let it advise mothers to watch over how their freewheeling sons are perceiving the external world. I suggest that the main duty of mothers is to bring children and men into the reality of the mother's human world, and that the duty of feminist philosophy is to explicate the logic behind this process.

The reality is that reason, especially mathematical reasoning, cannot arrive at any material conclusion whatsoever, whereas the mother's function is conclusive and real at all times. The materiality of the mother is her stock in trade and most essential characteristic, part and parcel of her ineluctable parturition, apogee of material being. What is wrong with cultural setups today is that mothers have been stripped of material wealth. The intrinsic value of woman's sexuality is all that is left to her, and if man could take that away too it seems that he would be pleased to do so. How funny it seems, then, that when we are sexually in love, we fight over mother and child *roles:* "If you're not strong, lean on me"; "whenever you need someone, let it be me"; "I'll be your baby tonight"; "I'll be your man tonight"; "I'll be your lady tonight"; "I'll be yours forever"; "I'll always care for you"; and so forth and so on, the unvarying *human theme* of *the strong caring for the weak* being unquenchable and unforgettable. Nonetheless, when *roles* turn into *functional realities,* the tunes change; now they become religious litanies of suffering with calls for mercy, feelingly sung from the distressed mother's viewpoint, the tragic Christ's viewpoint and *position* being not dissimilar to the mother's. God the father, the grantor of all favors, is now petitioned to deliver us. What stories these are! I think it is strictly up to mothers and feminist philosophers to retell them using a substantively more accurate content. In a short time, these retellings are bound to affect our art, our religious life, and our science.

Man desires woman's bodily embrace and woman *expects* man to desire her bodily embrace. I want to know, what is wrong with being loved *for our bodies alone?* Woman desires man's body as a *mother* surrogate, someone who will embrace her in a *human* fashion. In addition to that particular *human* comfort we all seek, we look for material wealth—assets we can draw upon to sustain us and make life more wonderful and entertaining. The mother fills the bill for many years but she cannot do it alone. She has either to scavenge from Nature or inspire sons and lovers to acquire wealth and *turn it over to her for dispensation.* Anyone who has experienced the misery of being hired help knows how unlikely it is we will turn over our hard-earned dollar to another person for dispensation. Herein lies a real conflict in man's intention towards woman. Is he the good provider or the resentful provider? Virginia Woolf wrote that woman to express herself *as a writer* needs money and a room of her own (she had an inherited income). Sexton had the support of middle class affluence, a husband, and two children, and she expressed herself in writing. Both of these widely-admired women committed suicide. The message seems to me writ rather large: unless woman accepts motherhood as the profoundest way on earth *to both understand and express oneself,* materiality counts for nought. Until conflicts in feminism are worked out along the lines of the human mother's cognition of her physical (sexual) largesse, her biological function, *and* the authority that runs concomitant with her parturition, feminism cannot move towards a feminist-oriented philosophy or science and the important questions surrounding our knowledge and constructs of the external world. Feminists insist that women are not and should never become "sex objects" for men but feminists as yet are far from comprehending the complexities of the *the mother's sexuality,* which is their own. I think we feminists must face up to those sexual and psychological complexities, peculiarly rooted in human motherhood and unrelated to fatherhood, before we can hope to find any way to achieve radical and overdue changes in our social practices.

I take the stand that our acquisition of knowledge concerning the external world depends upon the matriarchal, which is to say, the authoritative function of mothers, which function and authority cannot be simulated, for they derive from the personal cognition and self-knowledge of the knowing subject who is first and foremost the human mother. Matriarchy now lies buried under the economic tyranny of the patriarchs, who may or may not intend the best for their loved ones. Mankind *is* a load to carry and, sadly, wealth in the hands of men cannot carry us; wealth to be effective has to be in the possession of mothers for their discretionary use. Mothers who behave like spoiled children wreak havoc on families, and Sexton is a good case in point. Our technology cannot carry us, either, so long as it is under the control of men.

After females (and *males as well,* copying *mothers*) assume *intelligent maternal* control (in contradistinction to psychologically crazed or hysterical control) of our wealth and our technology, everything will be *done* differently. I see Woolf and Sexton as exceptional persons but it is the *norm* of motherhood that feminism must understand and explain to the young, girls and boys alike. *Most* mothers accept adulthood, its unglamorous responsibilities alongside nostalgic memories of childhood freedom. The essentialism of motherhood as a grand unifying theory will be accused *by feminists* of being retrogressive, a throwback to the feminine mystique of Mariolatry, the accepting agent who produces the perfect son of humble mother. Feminists should get off that tack and start thinking and teaching in memory of our *cognitively as well as sexually endowed mothers* instead of continually harping on impoverished, helpless, and victimized woman. If woman cannot start thinking in terms of motherhood as being the place where all *human* riches originate, which is to say all virtue, the species is lost.

Certainly there is supreme irony in the usurpation by men of the very notion of virtue, derived from the Latin *virtus* signifying manliness. Manliness naturally included strength, courage, and *excellence* (as understood by the Greek term *arete*). Virtue is always identified with knowledge, of ability to distinguish the difference between good and evil, right and wrong, an ability animals seem to do without with remarkable success. Why can't we? Plato complicated things by adding wisdom, temperance, and justice to the virtues of man. Aristotle distinguished between intellectual and moral virtues in man, holding that woman was incapable of either. The Stoics distinguished between theoretical and practical virtue, which sounds familiar, as does Augustine's insistence that love is the fundamental source of all virtue. Of course Augustine was referring to god's love and not to that of the human mother which so often disappoints and ultimately fails, but not so with god's. Who would not choose the more excellent, indeed the perfect love of god? Rousseau held virtue to be identified with following Nature, but famously backed off from defending this policy to its logical end of looking to woman for all virtue. Virtue for the very Protestant Kant related to duty: if we did our part by leading a moral and virtuous life, god would do his by somehow making commensurate human virtue and human happiness, if not in this life, then in another.

Scientific knowledge concerning the dynamics of the objectified universe delivers only technology to us, which may or may not prove beneficial. Besides, the *significance* of such knowledge to our lives is entirely missing. So among other things that feminism must accept viz female sexuality and gender is the fact that religion is here to stay, it being a deeper, more *applicable* insight into biological existence and our besotted begottenness than the broader, nicely cleaned up, rational humanism. The question, From what place? really reduces to, On what religious doctrine do we lean? We rely on convictions, on beliefs that to us seem true. The most profound of these beliefs are true of the human situation. We *see* them as being universally true for everyone, whatever the actual case may be. For all of these reasons, feminism must become a religion and there is little chance of that happening unless it is deeply grounded in the factual case, which I have argued is the venerable essentialism of motherhood. Knowledge works for us only if it affects our innermost being which certainly includes our sexuality, and nowhere is sexuality more universally observable than in man's physical connection to mothers and wives. The child screaming for its mother's teat is no less a form of sexual harassment than the husband demanding the right to copulate whether or not his wife is in the mood too. There is an alarming amount of talk among philosophers, scientists, and cognitive psychologists concerning the "power" of *technical* knowledge (especially neuroscience as the study of cognition) to increase *human* understanding in such a way as to solve our social problems. I see no way science can offer salvation to humanity unless we first understand the importance of the special *cognitive* knowledge human mothers alone are privy to.

Cognition frees woman from the blindness of dumb animalism, but the human mother's self-knowledge is far from liberating. On the contrary, with cognition comes the human mother's comprehension of how bound to Nature she is as well as how bound to herself children and men are. Scientific understanding of external world dynamics can be exhilarating *and* beneficial to the species only if the technology it makes possible proves to be of *direct* benefit to mothers. The exhilaration of scientific knowledge as power per se is sadistic and sick, in the same league as tying a can to a cat's tail simply to see what might happen.

Many feminists (and some men) view technology as virtually forcing a kind of mutation on our sexuality and experience of it. This, I have argued, is to undersell the essentialism of motherhood as nature's agency and not our own elected agency or god almighty's. Nature remains in charge of all things, including man's technology. To work with Nature is to work with motherhood. My muted theme has been: to work *religiously* with Nature is to work with motherhood. To comprehend Nature's mightiest force is to comprehend motherhood. To understand Nature is to understand the necessity of using and being used, of being exploited in full knowledge that that exploitation will be reappropriated by the exploited for her continuing glory. In religious analogy, that would be to claim that *motherhood* lives before and after particular mothers die after giving their lives that others might live. I have tried to make the points that by tapping into Nature we tap into the one who *provides* for us and that while Nature is our provident mother, she is not our *caring* mother. Only our partisan blood mother cares *especially* for us. Nature will not provide for us to her detriment, and neither in the long run will the blood mother.

My emphasis has been that the low self-esteem of human mothers today is the direct result of male attitudes reflecting the most misguided aspects of their "holy writ." I have held that it is these teachings feminism has the obligation to *displace with* healthier teachings, from which will come healthier attitudes towards motherhood and oneself, and new religious values. It is certainly more noble to love Nature than to love a mythical deity; it is unseemly and unworthy of human beings to *worship* anything. Mothers wouldn't dream of wanting to be worshipped; why some fathers dote on the idea is unfathomable except as an instrument of tyrannical power, which is abjectly unworthy and more accurately described as a pathology.

Although it seems irrational that one must die for others, the sense behind it is quite simple: the others are myself; there is no differentiation of any *kind* that can be made between *us:* human subject and human predicate; knowing subject and known object. Our differences have to do with time, place, and function. "I" is forever "I" and "you" is forever "you"; that is the imperishable mother/child construct of worldly reality and the basis of our syntactical language, Noam Chomsky notwithstanding. Spatially we occupy and know *about* the same one and only human world; but statistically as we go about *doing* our human world, our bodies are in different time phases of our specialized functions and our *minds* are probably in phases as disparate as our bodies. Feminism, I have insisted, must focus on the minds of mothers, for it is the mothers among us who will be doing the most realistic, the most imaginative, and the most socially applicable sort of intellectualizing. Moreover, mothers *know* that we die for you's. It is from that place of the sacrificing and sacrificed mother that feminist theory must be hypothesized. Just like technologized scientific knowledge, if feminism has nothing to offer mothers, it has nothing to offer anyone.

What feminism must offer *daughters* is Nietzsche's bold rallying cry: become what you are. And feminism must offer *sons* the same advice: become your mother (double intent), for that is too what you are and must become as best you can. The essential structure of biological reality cannot be put under the scientific microscopic eye. Only under the intelligent mother's eye can it be viewed with clarity and understanding. Whether the eye behind the microscope sees through female or male eyes is far from an uninteresting question, but for *theory* concerning the uniquely human *system* one must turn to the mother's gaze upon her child. At birth, the child knows everything there is to know about the bliss of total custodial care. The mother can remember that, too, but she also now possesses considerable predictive powers concerning her fate as well as the fate of her children. If the child is a son, she sees one fate, if it is a daughter, she quite rightly sees another: the fate of the sacrificed. Should she teach her daughter to be sacrificed willingly, and help her to understand the deep sacredness of sacrifice, or should she recoil in horror at her darling daughter being offered up to a seemingly unintelligible destiny? What can she do to prevent it? Teach Women's Studies to young ladies, writing the curriculum herself and taking care that it includes the options of careers and peerage with children and men, and no sacrificial motherhood?

It shouldn't have to be argued that there's no concrete laboratory high enough nor genetic engineering adroit enough to contain Nature and her natural ways. I have tried to draw a picture showing that, as always, Nature and females will work with the present moment, with what is here. Man anyway doesn't know what to do with the technology he has created, or with himself. He is playing only a game while waiting for dinner to be announced or for Mom to burst in and break it up. Women entering science, academe, the military, the church, and finally writing and publishing like pros, seems promising. But unless we make our presence known as *functioning mothers* with more on our minds than pleasant pastimes, cushy jobs, handsome recompense, prestige and privilege, then the species will continue to deteriorate. Though mothers prove often mistaken and misguided, we never outgrow our need for them; their intentions are what must be studied and never underestimated. Our total dependence upon *authorities* in all disciplines goes back to our reliance upon the authority of mothers. Call mothers gluttons for punishment or what you will, but it is Nature's own way. Motherhood can only succeed, regardless of how many individual mothers fail. By one route or another the essential structure of motherhood holds, rebuilding and renewing itself as it goes along according to what it is destined to do. (Feminists must always keep in mind that destiny does not imply a destination.)

I have not harped on the perhaps unwelcome fact that what the mother knows cannot liberate her, cannot change her destiny, cannot put her in control of her essential system, her motherhood. Since the essence of motherhood is immutable, the best example in the universe of an eternal form, what woman knows allows her only to speak to and instruct her offspring concerning certain social behavioral practices. One of these instructions to the son is to "behave like a man." Now it is left for feminist mothers to relay to sons and lovers what it is to behave like a man. That is, after feminist professors in Women's Studies have caught on to the importance of underscoring to young ladies that they must behave like responsible and authoritative mothers. To be a man is to be a credit to one's mother (again the Jewish mother's the one who has it right). To be a mother is to be a benign monarch, an authoritative philosopher do-gooder, a super rational humanist, a tragic figure acutely aware of her unfixable flaw, a feminist. It is to be no longer a child. I hope I've shown that the mother possesses the *only* authoritative voice well able to contradict the authority and very name of the father.

Feminists seem unable to agree upon a single premise from which all must work. That location it seems to me is well marked by every "struggling" mother with child. I've never before become so weary of a term as I have now become with "struggle." It is used as a trope in almost any reference to women: struggling women and women struggling, the struggle of feminists, and the struggling feminist movement, etc. Academic feminists are putting on airs when they speak of struggling to be heard; many mothers privately making radical decisions to free themselves of domineering spouses and to exert their own authoritative voices in dealings with their children began the rumble that was eventually heard worldwide as a woman's movement of disquiet. If academic feminists persist in speaking as "struggling" scholars instead of as competent and intelligent mothers, they won't be seen as doing much to inspire the world's mothers to radicalize social norms. More's the pity if they inspire the world's mothers to give up motherhood and to become scholars instead. I have tried to sound this warning.

Remember, there is nothing more futile than to suppose that a perfect explanation can be found for anything. Awareness of this simple fact keeps mothers from putting on airs about how much we, sadly, know. The Enlightenment's main mistake was in believing that reality has a structure that perfect reason (once perfected) can discover. The originary human mother reasoned very differently. She reasoned that it is the essential structure of biological reality that has been perfected by Nature and that even woman's understanding of this structure no doubt is far from perfected. Yet, significantly, the mother's grasp of life's biological structure far exceeds the child's or the manchild's. It is no wonder male empiricists have stayed away from these intimate sexual experiences from which we learn so much. But why do feminist empiricists insist on stepping around them? I've suggested that many intelligent mothers now see that putting too much store in the education of sons has, in the long run, worked to our detriment. It was only an experiment, and for a while it appeared to be a great solution to woman's overburdened public life. Worldwide, mothers are probably now fuller of inventive new solutions than academic feminists ever dreamed of. I was dismayed to find no clue that academic feminists are looking for data at the source of where it's happening, among schooled and unschooled mothers, instead of in the bogs of intramural academic discourse and jealous infighting for public acclaim and elitist prestige, just like academic men. I'm sure some of the authors are mothers, but they did not *speak as mothers*. My intent has been to jolt these self-proclaimed feminists to speak as *mothers*. Mothers *identify* with other mothers. We usually talk about *children,* and try to offer helpful advice to one another. We find that most often our problems are similar if not identical; we can laugh together and we can bond and feel in community with one another as a community of long-suffering *mothers*.

Beyond question, the mother's voice of authority has been squeezed out by the divine voice and authority of the name of the father which to this day remains embedded in a pre-enlightenment metaphysics. The unwillingness of males to give up the worldly privileges which this metaphysics guarantees them is explanation enough of the male habit of concentrating on anything on earth or in the heavens, seen or unseen, anything, anything, except the facts of biology, sexuality, and gender. Man may be willing to ignore the centrality of the mother but it is there, to her place, that he must repair when his barren technologized, war-ridden world becomes intolerable. I don't think it ever occurs to males that females might not be *there, t*he place of escape, when things become too terrible to face. But it's frightening to think that feminists are committing the same arrogance in camping with the "free"; freedom's assumption is that *someone* will always be *there* but I fear it's not likely to be us unless human mothers who know what they're doing stick to their cognitive guns.

Academic feminists do appear to be evincing concern for some of the nitty gritty details of human existentiality, but nowhere is the question brought up that the mother's authentic authority *logically* takes precedence over the authority of the name of the father, and for the soundest of reasons. My intent has been to explain the logic and to give the reasons. In the hands of men, the scientific method may be intrinsically incapable of doing what it was supposedly constructed to do, namely displace metaphysics as a way of knowing, but this intrinsic incapability has to do with man's unwillingness (whether he be scientist or the pope) to relinquish access to woman's body *on his terms.* Many adult males have no genuine interest in woman's body; presumably the pope would be a good example. That does not keep such males from bonding with men who do. Men bond together against women because men and children abhor the thought that access to the mother should be on *her terms.* I argue that men *hate* civilization and *peace.* For instance, they actually believe that a righteous war is among the most civilized activities the world has known. Brothers *love* killing their brothers, that is, so long as there is a Big Brother (read dethroned mother) in the wings, watching and eager to assure them they fought *bravely* and to reward them with kisses, medals, public homage, and ceremonies that make *everyone* glad that we are strong and intelligent enough to kill certain brothers when the necessity arises. The lack of fit between the experiences of mothers and the "dominant conceptual schemes" of men has much to do with the metaphysical scheme of the divine authority of the name of the father. I do not think mothers are alienated from their own experience by the dominant male "conceptual schemes" but *accepting the interpretation* of woman's place in the "divine" plan lessens the likelihood that such mothers will become raging feminists.

I have spent a lot of time reading what feminists are writing, and I think I see what they see and describe quite well, often in meticulous detail. But since so little is said concerning the efficacious place of motherhood in these writings, I find feminist analyses disheartening to read. They seem grounded more in wordiness (for example, modernism, postmodernism, scientific objectivism, transcendent ideals of the enlightenment, deconstruction, literary criticism, and so on) than rooted in any physical model of how the female system works, biologically and socially. What I see and describe as Nature's transcendent methodology of motherhood surely could be seen and described differently, and that would be no devastation of what I see and am trying to relay descriptively. The end purpose of asking, Do you see what I see? is always the hope of consensus. Among mothers, the inquiry, Do you do what I do? is unnecessary. Among fathers, it is a necessary question. Among feminists it is futile to ask, Do you see what I see or Do you do what I do, unless they are addressing women and asking as mothers, with the *intention* of reaching a new consensus concerning social praxis.

Even should consensus among feminists, women, and mothers be reached after much exchange of thesis and antithesis, motherhood does not function dialectically, although fatherhood seems somehow to have managed, indeed perfected, something of the sort, "historically" speaking. Fatherhood has a social history based more or less on dialectics but motherhood transcends history and the theory of evolution itself. One cannot encounter or imagine the appearance of anything without inquiring about its source, where it came from, and its method of appearing in one's life or path. Children and men are loath to imagine where mothers come from; to them we are a given. But it is quite easy for mothers to figure out where children and men come from, although they too are a given in the life of woman. Woman too may be loath to examine her own life. To the put-upon mother, perhaps only an unexamined life seems liveable at all. In any case, I am convinced that the ordinary mother does not think in terms of history nor attach much value to it if "educated." I also consider this a very intelligent attitude. Many educated feminists, after taking a look at motherhood, elect to join the ranks of men in efforts to write and rewrite history. The political ideal of feminists is declared to be one of inclusiveness, that is, to be *included with men* in history, especially histories yet to be written; but the inclusion is to be as individual *persons,* not as authoritative *mothers* and humankind's only *model figures.* I see this sort of ambition as yet another example of the child's desire to become an adult and escape the embrace of the mother's *authority.* Daughter and son alike passionately desire to escape the mother's transcendent *authority* over every aspect of their lives.

How little we know, until motherhood itself teaches us! Motherhood *as Nature* counts for the next generation, not whatever acquired belief can be pumped into the present generation as permanent "knowledge." The heuristic of motherhood is thus always more physical than dialectical. While fathering is also a physical act, the heuristic of fatherhood is worked out by man according to a dialectic which he himself applies to "his" history. Man believes that his own authority, held in the name of the father, is the sole means by which human existence will be perfected, all in good time. Not only does such "reasoning" reflect the enormous hubris underpinning dialectics as historical process; it is to presume a knowledge of what constitutes perfection. The transparency of this childlike innocence reveals the situate difference between the mother's place and experience, and the child's place and experience. Ergo, if childhood is more desirable than adulthood, especially if one happens to be female and destined for motherhood, why not make of that situate an *ideal* goal for which to strive, and eventually attain? The sensibilities of adult males

—monarchs, priests, philosophers, scientists, professors, legislators—are gravely offended at any suggestion that they not only might not know, but might have little if any *intention* of doing what is best for mankind. Unless feminists tie in their concerns and recommendations with the concerns and *needs* of mothers, feminist sensibilities and intentions will soon be as suspect as the sensibilities and intentions of men. Feminists are already showing their own brand of touchiness concerning any challenge to the real motives behind their academic concerns.

If one believes in the child, one must necessarily believe in motherhood. It is not necessary to believe in fatherhood. To believe in motherhood also necessitates believing in the agency and authority of mothers. Belief in and reliance upon the biological necessity of insemination in no way necessitates a belief in and reliance upon the authority or the name of the father. A full reassertion of maternal authority would soon result in mothers reclaiming the land, occupying all governmental offices, presiding over all religious ceremonies, directing all educational programs, and not least, heading the military. Most men, I believe, would adjust happily, so long as they were included along with the children and provided with enough games and sports to keep them preoccupied and out of mischief. Man's current violence and rage against woman seems to be a result of her inability to care for him properly. It is the rage of the broken promise. With all assets and amenities under the control of mothers, men should fare better. Normally we attach allegiance to the person or entity that cares for us and the child loves the mother for no other reason. The mother reciprocates the child's love but not for the same reason, the child being totally unable to care in any helpful way for the mother.

Why do mothers love children and men? What reason? The reason is that they belong to us; they are our most valuable property and as such we must care for them and as mothers we do, giving them our utmost attention. Usually we do not love paid servants, since we do not own them; and slaves are viewed as unworthy of any human regard. I doubt that mothers would ever own slaves; that seems a manchild's way of reasoning, since children and men gladly enslave mothers and most expect to do so as a matter of course. Mothers who accept such tyranny have only themselves to blame. Those mothers who do not feel tyrannized can always fall back on Hegel's ineluctable master and servant paradigm which maps nicely onto *religious* paradoxes of the servant being greater than the master, and the last at some point coming miraculously first. However, both the religiose and the secularized versions of this paradigm are transparently sentimental rather than analytical. The servant and the served properly refer to the mother and the child, and *my point is* that the child is *not* master or mistress of the mother.

According to Kant, who is considered to be the past master of human reasoning, the motto of enlightenment is Dare to Know. Men have always equated to know with the power to control. Mothers more often have equated to know with to sorrow and to suffer. Nevertheless, motherhood is instituted by Nature and fatherhood is instituted and legitimized only by the "word" of god. God's word has been rewritten a number of times and can be rewritten many more. Illumination by the divine word of the father stands in dark contrast to illumination by experience coupled with an intellectual capacity and unflinching *willingness* to reason. To judge by the numbers of feminists fleeing any serious thought regarding the essentialism of motherhood, I'm afraid feminists are not so daring or brave or intellectually willing to seek and find out as they imagine themselves to be. Never mind, without seeking, mothers find out anyway and they are the authorities to whom we must address our inquiries if we want to learn about knowledge, truth, and mercy, if not about justice (I've never known anyone who wanted to learn firsthand about justice).

To me, it's obvious that the many questions surrounding notions of a priori truth can be discussed most convincingly from the human mother's *perception of her situation and function* during parturition. With the biological appearance of offspring, where there was one, a series of one's phenomenally appears. Epistemologies involving a Kantian-type intuition can serve feminist philosophy well, as soon as philosophical, scientific, and mathematical disciplines include modern women and men possessing a biologically comprehensive understanding of motherhood. A correct understanding of motherhood will effect a rerooting of our human knowledge in the ground of our human experience, rather than in words and ideological values, including the ideologies of "pure" reason and "pure" mathematical knowledge. The function of that term "pure" has been to exclude from philosophy and science any taint of woman's unsavory sexual knowledge and the bald facts concerning discrete individuations that go with it. As Kant learned after much tortured reasoning, there is no escape from a certain dynamic One, from which number Two is derived. Those unitary two's, and *any quantity* or aggregate of them, remain forever connected to the dynamism of a *specific* number One, the source of their being. There is no unconstrained autonomy in the entire universe and trying to reason otherwise is what drove Kant and Hegel into metaphysics, and Nietzsche crazy; it drives mathematicians and logicians, who deal in symbols and modal logic, into insolvable paradoxes. In the game of *real numbers,* which is to say, in *life,* the solution is death: only in case the knowing subjects regularly die can innocent, unknowledgeable neophytes move up and take their place, to learn firsthand and to their horror all about the blood bath life turns out to be. In the theatre, this is precisely what tragedians dare us to know. The Protestant Kant was no tragedian.

As far as humanity goes, I finally conclude that, should human motherhood prove itself cognitively dysfunctional, the human world comes to a close. The creaturely world is comprised primarily of dumb females who live in a real world with dumb males. Not a one of them understands what's going on, and it doesn't matter a bit so far as the quality of their lives is concerned. If the human female's cognition of her own sexuality fails to help her enrich the quality of her own life in particular and the human community's life in general, then intelligence itself is a failure. To date, a lot of evidence seems to point to the conclusion that human intelligence fails whereas blind, unintelligent randomness succeeds. Over the longest overview that human mothers can intelligently take, distinguishing between success and failure begins to seem rather precious, except for the important questions, asked as usual by men: what's for dinner tonight?; will I be seeing you?

Bibliography

Hall, Pamela. "Feminism and the Canon." In *The Journal of Philosophy,* Vol. LXXXVIII, No. 10, October 1991, p. 568.

Hirsch, Marianne, and Keller, Evelyn Fox, eds. *Conflicts in Feminism*. New York: Routledge, 1990.

Jones, Kathleen B. "The Trouble with Authority." In *Differences,* Vol. 5, No. 1, Spring 1991, pp. 104-127.

Kitcher, Patricia. *Kant's Transcendental Psychology*. New York: Oxford University Press, 1990.

Kitcher, Philip. *The Nature of Mathematical Knowledge*. New York: Oxford University Press, 1984.

Kittay, Eva Feder. "In Whose Different Voice?" In *The Journal of Philosophy,* Vol. LXXXVIII, No. 11, November 1991, pp. 645-646.

Kourany, Janet A. "Philosophy in a Different Voice." In *The Journal of Philosophy,* Vol. LXXXVIII, No. 10, October 1991, pp. 557-567.

Lacan, Jacques. *The Four Fundamental Concepts of Psycho-Analysis*. New York: W.W. Norton & Company, 1981.

Longino, Helen. "Multiplying Subjects and the Diffusion of Power." In *The Journal of Philosophy,* Vol. LXXXVIII, No. 11, November 1991, pp. 666-674.

Minow, Martha. "Equalities." In *The Journal of Philosophy,* Vol. LXXXVIII, No. 11, November 1991, pp. 633-644.

Rouse, Joseph. "The Dynamics of Power of Knowledge in Science." In *The Journal of Philosophy*, Vol. LXXXVIII, No. 11, November 1991, pp. 658-665.

Index

About the Author

Rebecca Boone is a retired journalist and editor living in Berkeley, California, and an active mother and grandmother. Her *A Philosophy of Woman* was published in 1984.